A Clove of GARLIC

A Clove of GARLIC

Garlic for Health and Cookery: Recipes and Traditions

KATY HOLDER
AND
GAIL DUFF

CHARTWELL BOOKS, INC.

A QUARTO BOOK

Published by Chartwell Books
a division of Book Sales Inc.
114 Northfield Avenue
Edison, New Jersey 08837

This edition is produced for sale in the USA,
its territories and dependencies only.

ISBN 0-7858-0894-9

This book was designed and produced by
Quarto Publishing plc
The Old Brewery
6 Blundell Street
London N7 9BH

Senior editors: Michelle Pickering, Sian Parkhouse
Senior art editor: Clare Baggaley
Copy editors: Mary Senechal, Deborah Savage
Designer: Allan Mole
Photographer: David Sherwin
Stylist: Maureen Kane
Photographer's assistant: Lee Patterson
Home economist: Katy Holder
Illustrators: Jane Smith, Valerie Price, Steve Tse
Picture researcher: Susannah Jayes
Picture manager: Giulia Hetherington
Art director: Moira Clinch
Editorial director: Mark Dartford

Typeset in Great Britain by Central Southern Typesetters, Eastbourne
Manufactured in Hong Kong by Regent Publishing Services Ltd
Printed in Hong Kong by Sing Cheong Printing Co. Ltd.

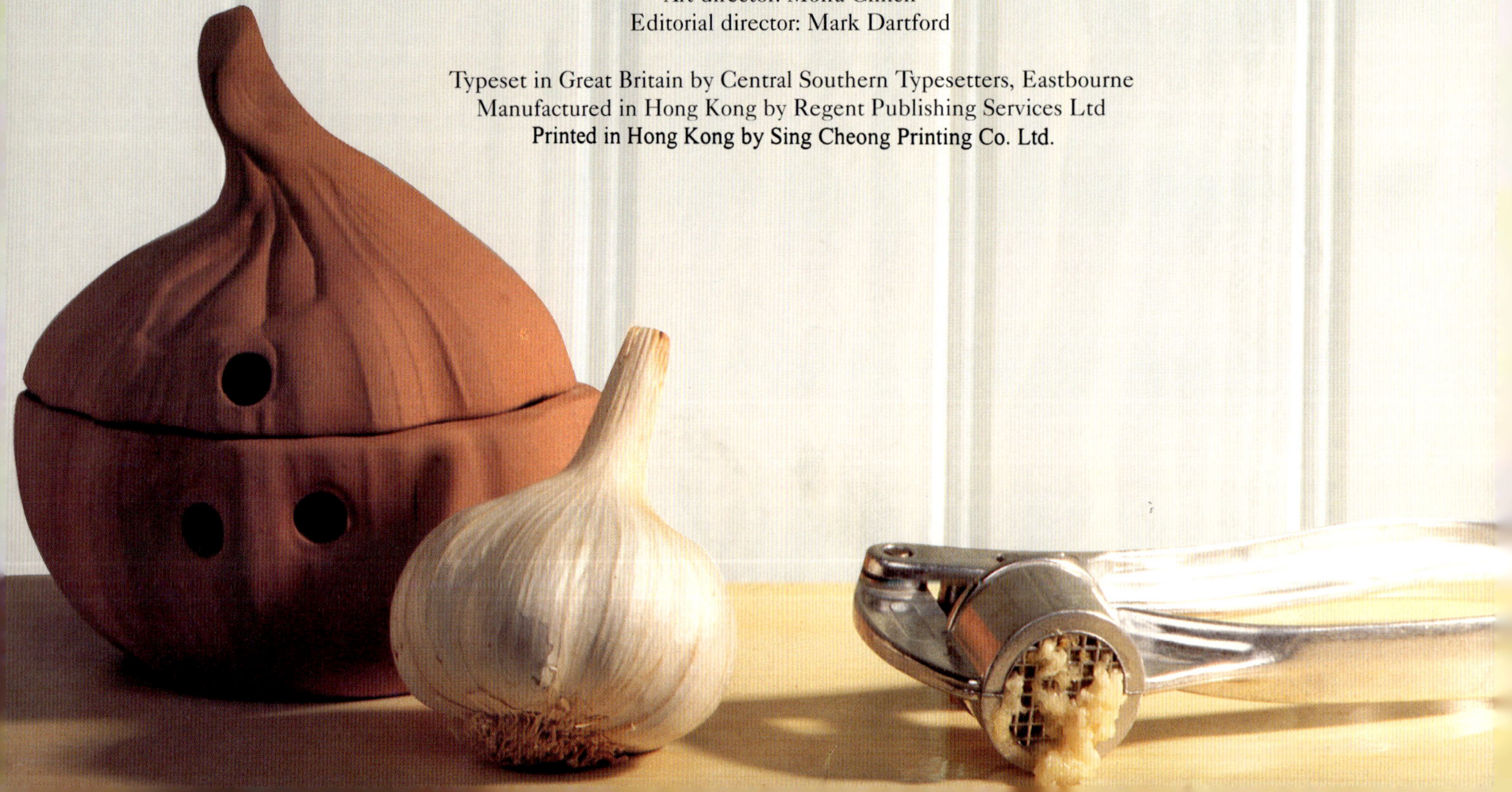

Contents

INTRODUCTION

THERE CANNOT BE ANY PLANT PEOPLE HAVE LOVED OR DISLIKED SO MUCH AS GARLIC. IT ADDS SAVOR TO FOOD; ITS VERY SMELL PROMOTES GOOD APPETITE; ITS NUMEROUS MEDICINAL QUALITIES HAVE CAUSED IT TO BE REGARDED AS A MIRACLE CURE-ALL; IT HAS SERVED AS A PROTECTION AGAINST EVIL. BUT THERE IS A PRICE TO PAY—GARLIC BREATH! SOMETHING SO SPECIAL CANNOT BE COMPLETELY PERFECT, AFTER ALL!

Wild garlic growing in the woods make a pretty sight in summer when the heads of white flowers appear. They can also be detected by their smell from some way off.

Garlic is indeed a special plant. It is easy to cultivate and can be grown in temperate and hot climates, both commercially and in private gardens and tubs. It is relatively cheap to buy in stores and markets when compared weight for weight with other herbs and spices. If you grow it in quantity, it will store well for several months, and there is nothing complicated about its preparation for cooking or medicinal use. Garlic is therefore available to everyone: the "Poor Man's Theriac [Cure-All]," as it was once called, later corrupted to Poor Man's Treacle.

The history of garlic goes back a very long way. Native to Central Asia, it was soon transported around the world by wandering tribesmen, conquerors, tradesmen, and explorers. Five thousand years ago garlic was grown in China. The ancient Egyptians ate quantities of it, the Romans took it to northern Europe, Columbus introduced it to Central and South America, and later settlers carried it to what is now the United States.

In many cultures garlic has been almost as important for flavoring as salt, and yet each cuisine retains its own style and its own basic flavors. For example, the fiery African condiment berbere and the smooth French garlic soup. This shows

This illustration from a French manuscript shows a field of garlic being harvested. The bulbs are tied into bunches ready for storing.

garlic's versatility as an ingredient, and demonstrates—despite arguments to the contrary—that it has a complementary rather than dominant flavor.

Garlic's powers as a medicine have also long been praised, and current research suggests that some of the old beliefs about it are true. Garlic can help to treat infections, particularly those of the respiratory tract. It can help to lower blood pressure, improve the circulation and combat the build-up of cholesterol. It can strengthen our resistance to viral infections and common bugs which cause food poisoning. It is also a natural antiseptic.

Garlic's alleged magical powers cannot be overlooked. Widely known as a safeguard against illnesses, garlic has also been used for protection from demons and vampires. It was so holy in ancient Egypt that oaths were sworn on its name; in Greece, it was sacred to the goddess Hecate. Eating it was thought to make you strong and brave.

The popularity of garlic has swung backward and forward over the centuries. Sometimes revered for its healing and flavoring properties, sometimes thought to be too vulgar for the upper classes because of its odor, garlic has never been loved by all of the people all of the time. In the United States and Britain, for example, it was hardly used at all in the early years of the 20th century.

Now, however, garlic has come into its own. Faster, cheaper travel has led to a global exchange of cuisines and flavors; a search for natural cures in a synthetic age has meant that serious research has been done into the properties of herbs; and an increasing desire for a spiritual dimension in their lives has meant that more people are looking at the customs and beliefs of other cultures and of the ancient world. Garlic is a worldwide food ingredient, it is a valued healing plant, and it has an established place in religion, myth, and magic. Its time has most certainly come.

History

Loved for its health-giving and culinary properties, though sometimes despised for its smell, garlic has been one of the world's most useful plants for the past six thousand years.

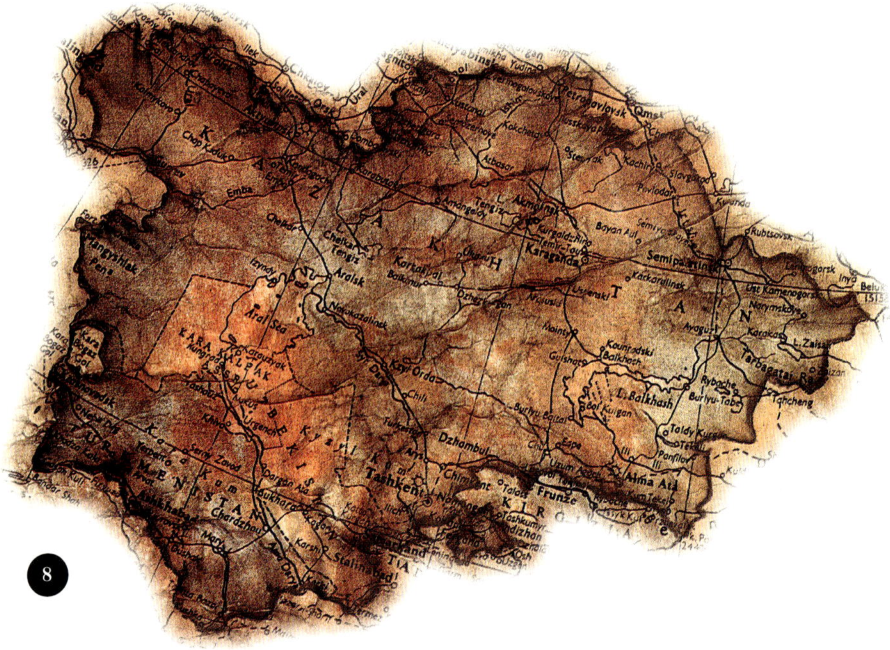

This map shows the republics of Turkmenistan, Kazakhstan, and Uzbekistan in southwestern Siberia, where garlic is believed to have originated.

Because garlic was introduced to a large number of cultures almost simultaneously and at an early stage in history, many countries claim it as their own. However, it probably originated in southwestern Siberia and in what are now the republics of Turkmenistan, Kazakhstan, and Uzbekistan, where it still grows wild.

Garlic is easy to grow and keep and the plants are productive, which helped its rapid spread from its original habitat. Five thousand years ago nomadic tribes carried it to China, where it quickly became widely used. From there it spread to Southeast Asia. By 2000 B.C. garlic had journeyed through the Middle East to Egypt, and from there it went with traders and travelers all the way across southern Europe, becoming naturalized in Sicily. It also spread down through India, where it was mentioned in the earliest Vedic writings, ancient religious scripts found in eastern India.

Phoenician traders shipped garlic a little farther north into southern Europe, and the Romans took it into every region they conquered, including Britain and northern Europe. Later, the Vikings carried garlic on their many long sea voyages around the globe. Columbus brought it to what is now the Dominican Republic and from there it spread across Central and South America to become naturalized in North America.

Back where it started, in Siberia and around the Caspian Sea, garlic was a valuable commodity. As late as the 18th century, the Siberians could pay their government taxes in garlic: 15 bulbs for a man; 10 for a woman; and 5 for each child.

Garlic is now cultivated all over the world, and there is hardly a food store or restaurant without it. Despite its consistent popularity in many cultures, however, in others garlic has swung in and out of favor down the ages,

This illustration from a medieval German manuscript shows the reaping of the harvest. Meat and fish were of limited availability and garlic helped to give variety to the mainly vegetarian diet.

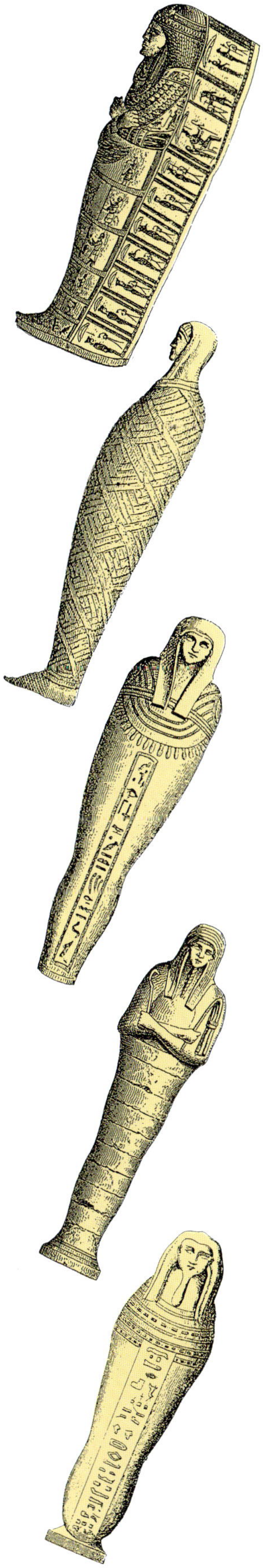

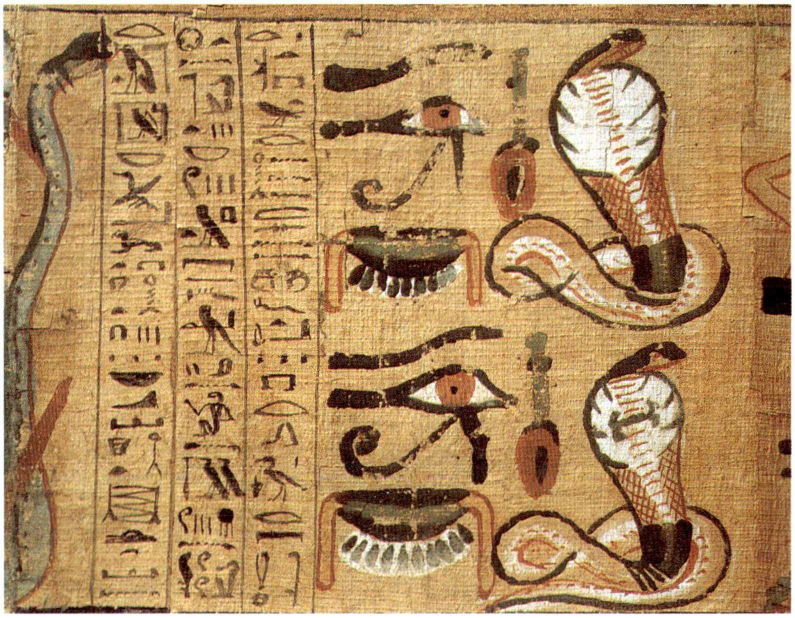

By 2000 B.C. garlic was being grown in Egypt. Highly valued, it was placed alongside the mummified bodies of the dead (left) to sustain them in the afterlife. The 21st-Dynasty Book of the Dead *(right), a scroll papyrus, contained 800 herbal remedies, of which 22 mentioned garlic.*

largely because of its smell—or, more correctly, the smell that it imparts to the eater's breath. Even while its healing, health-giving, and flavoring properties continued to be acknowledged, its unsociable side-effect sometimes confined it to the diet of those regarded as the "lower orders."

Garlic in Ancient Times

The first written reference to garlic comes from the Sumerian culture, 5,000 years ago, in a document describing foods and crops. The Sumerians were efficient farmers and food producers, living in what is now the Middle East, who grew a wide variety of crops in accordance with the principle that land producing grains and legumes would feed more people than land grazed by animals. They therefore ate very little meat, and garlic added flavor to an otherwise plain diet of grains, legumes, and fresh vegetables.

In the same period, garlic became part of Chinese cooking, and was combined with young, green onions, ginger, and soy sauce to produce the characteristic flavor of Chinese food which we still recognize today.

The ancient pyramids at Giza were built by laborers who received daily rations of onions, garlic, and bread.

The famed Greek poet Homer praised the medicinal properties of garlic.

"Here it is recorded how much black radish, red onion and garlic went to the workers."

HERODOTUS, GREEK HISTORIAN, *c.*484–425 B.C.

The ancient Egyptians adored garlic. They ate it raw and cooked, and believed that it nourished the spirit as well as the body. Garlic was used in mummification, and garlic bulbs—both real and made of clay—were placed in tombs for the deceased to use in the afterlife. Pharaoh Cheops issued the pyramid builders with daily garlic rations to give them strength and prevent them from catching infectious diseases which could stop them working. An inscription on the pyramid at Giza states how much garlic and onions was consumed by the men who built it. When the ration was cut, they went on strike; free garlic was a valuable perk. Weight for weight, a slave was worth less than garlic, for an Egyptian slave could be bought with just 15 pounds of the bulbs.

The Hebrews, living alongside the Egyptians for so many years, came to value garlic just as much. When Moses led them into the desert and all they had was manna, they complained loudly: "We remember . . . the cucumbers, and the melons, and the leeks, and the onions, and the garlic" (Numbers XI:5). Much later, in Roman times, the Jewish people still maintained this affection for garlic, which earned them the nickname of "the stinking ones"—an unjustified slur since the Romans used almost as much of it themselves.

Our love of garlic today is just as great as in classical times. In "The Stinking Rose" restaurants almost every dish contains it.

The ancient Greeks seem to have entertained the same love-hate relationship with garlic that many people have today. They called it the "stinking rose," and Greeks who had been eating garlic were forbidden to enter the temple of Cybele. Nevertheless vast quantities were consumed. According to Homer, writing in the 8th century B.C., garlic was part of a feast served by the Trojan war hero Nestor to his guest Machaon.

By 300 B.C., the sophisticated Greeks of Athens had developed their own form of minimalist eating, and before each meal they served a selection of small hors d'oeuvres. The writer Lunceus, in a work called *The Centaur*, complained this was not the sort of dinner for a hungry man: "For the cook sets before you a large tray on which there are five small plates. One of these holds garlic, another a pair of sea urchins, another a sweet wine sop, another ten cockles, the last a small piece of sturgeon."

Working people in ancient Greece ate garlic not as a fashionable fad, but to spice up their everyday foods and also to give them strength and resistance to disease. Homer, Aristotle, and Hippocrates all praised garlic's medicinal qualities. Greek soldiers, athletes, and wrestlers were said to eat large quantities of it to provide strength, courage, and endurance, and it was always included in Greek military supplies.

In Rome, too, garlic was both medicine and food, loved always by the ordinary people, but on occasions scorned by the upper classes who, like the poet Horace, called it vulgar. The well-known writer and gastronome Alexandre Dumas, wrote in 1873 of Horace's experiences with garlic: "Horace, who suffered indigestion on the very day of his arrival in Rome, from a sheep's head prepared with garlic, had a horror of it." One suspects the cause to have been the sheep's head rather than the garlic, but it apparently put him off for life and he later called garlic "more poisonous than hemlock."

Roman soldiers, like their Greek counterparts, received regular garlic rations, and they sowed the plant wherever they went. To them, and to farm workers, it was a powerful tonic, maintaining strength and combating infection. It was unusual to find a Roman soldier without

This pavement mosaic shows Roman soldiers journeying down the Nile. Like the Egyptians, the Romans loved garlic and believed that it was a strength-giving tonic.

Substitute for Salt Fish: Pound as much cumin as you can pick up with five fingers, half the quantity of pepper, and one peeled clove of garlic. Pour on liquamen [fish sauce], add a few drops of oil. This is excellent for a sick stomach and facilitates digestion.

APICIUS
THE ROMAN COOKERY BOOK, 1ST CENTURY A.D.

his garlic, and any tender young recruit from the aristocracy was told, when on his way to enlist, *Allia ne comedas* ("Don't eat the garlic"). He probably did, and was probably all the healthier, since its medicinal virtues were praised by physicians such as Dioscorides and by the writers Virgil and Pliny.

In Roman cooking, garlic was used for sauces and for salad dressings. The cookbook of Apicius contains a recipe for *Sala Cattabia*, a dressing for a salad of meat and vegetables. It includes bread crumbs soaked in water and vinegar and pounded with garlic, honey, mint, coriander, pepper, cheese, and oil. Another favorite was *moretum*, a sustaining mixture of pounded garlic, cheese rind, and herbs.

While the Greeks and Romans were enjoying the virtues of garlic, the Scythians roamed the fertile plains around the Caspian and Black seas in wagons, following their migrating herds of cattle. The Greek physician Hippocrates wrote that they were a fat and humorous people. Their diet consisted of animal and dairy products, tuna fish, and sturgeon, and onions, garlic, and beans, which they grew when staying on their summer pastures.

In Britain and northern Europe, before the arrival of the Romans, Iron Age settlers sought out field garlic and wild garlic, which grew in damp woods. *Allium sativum*, which is the species that we know today, must have been a

Hippocrates, the ancient Greek physician considered to be the founder of modern medicine, relied heavily on garlic as a pain killer. He used a mixture of opium taken from poppies, garlic juice, and wine, and found this potion to be effective both for patients requiring surgery and for those suffering from wounds.

Wherever they traveled, Roman soldiers carried garlic with them. This Roman mosaic shows a hunting scene on the banks of the Nile. Both the Romans and the native Egyptians would have used garlic to flavor most of their meat dishes.

Wild garlic, growing in damp woodlands, would have been a familiar sight in Anglo-Saxon times in England.

welcome addition to any stewpot bubbling over the fire, and when the Romans left around A.D. 300, garlic remained.

Garlic During the Middle Ages

In Anglo-Saxon England, garlic was listed in manuscripts as one of the six onion types. Known as *garleac*, it appeared alongside *cropleac* (everlasting onions or chives), *porleac* (leek), *ynioleac* (onions), *bol-leac*, and *brae-leac* (other members of the onion family, probably similar to scallions).

Meanwhile, garlic retained its supremacy throughout the Middle East. It was praised by the prophet Mohammed and consequently

Here capers grace a sauce vermilion
Whose fragrant odors to the soul are blown…
Here pungent garlic meets the eager sight
And whets with savor sharp appetite,
While olives turn to shadowed night the day,
And salted fish in slices rims the tray.

IBN AL-MU'TAZZ, ISLAMIC POET, 10TH CENTURY

Charlemagne, the emperor of France and the Holy Roman Empire in the 8th and 9th centuries, ordered garlic to be grown in the gardens of all his properties.

featured among first courses served in the court of the Caliphs of Baghdad.

In France, garlic was adopted with particular and enduring delight. The French emperor Charlemagne (747–814) advised his subjects to grow it. Throughout the Middle Ages the plant could be found flourishing in monastery gardens all over Europe.

From the 10th to the 16th centuries, garlic featured in most English horticultural papers and books. Sometimes it was praised and sometimes scorned, one writer listing it alongside drunkenness and late eating as "hurtful to the brain." Garlic cloves were rubbed over bread which was eaten at the beginning of a drinking session; and sometimes they were steeped in red wine in an attempt to counter the effects of alcohol.

Peasants all over Europe, Britain included, chewed garlic to keep away infections and act as a general tonic. Beton the brewer-woman, a

> "Do not eat garlic or onions; for their smell will reveal that you are a peasant."
>
> CERVANTES, *DON QUIXOTE*, 1614

character in *Piers Plowman* (written *c.*1365), names garlic, pepper, peony seed, and fennel seed as the "hot spices" grown and used by the ordinary people. The rich could import spices, but the poor had to grow their own, and garlic was easy to cultivate.

Garlic sauce was often eaten with goose. Alexander Neckam, in the 12th century, recommended a strong garlic sauce made with wine or verjuice (the sour juice of crab-apples or grapes) to go with a "stubble" goose (fattened by gleaning on the stubble after the harvest). The association with goose was still alive 400 years later, when Thomas Mouffet remarked, "If a goose be eaten above four months old, it is badly digested without garlic sauce, exercise and strong drink." Was the garlic culinary or medicinal? It was probably a bit of both.

The appearance of garlic in various cooking manuscripts of the early 14th century, shows the favor it then enjoyed with the upper classes. It was listed as one of the 47 "green herbs for pottage," or stew, which included dandelions, marigolds, daisies, red nettle, lettuce, chives, leeks, rape, and radishes. In a book called *The Forme of Cury*, there is one of the earliest salad recipes:

SALAT

Take persel [PARSLEY], *sawge* [SAGE], *grene garlic* [IE THE GREEN TOPS OF THE PLANT], *chibolles* [GREEN ONIONS OR SCALLIONS], *oynouns* [ONIONS], *leek, borage, myntes, porettes, fennel, and toun cressis* [TOWN CRESSES], *rew* [RUE], *rosmarye, purslarye* [PURSLAINE]; *wasche hem clene. Pike hem* [PICK THEM OVER]. *Pluck hem small with thyn honde, and myng* [MIX] *hem wel with rawe oile; lay on vinegar and salt, and serve it forth.*

In medieval Britain, garlic had the reputation of being eaten only by vulgar people, such as the Summoner in Chaucer's Prologue to The Canterbury Tales. *This illustration is taken from the Ellesmere edition of the book.*

The same book contains a recipe for *Chykens in hocchee* [broth]. The chickens are stuffed with a mixture of garlic, grapes, parsley, and sage, simmered in broth and served sprinkled with sweet mixed spices.

In Spain at this time, however, Alfonso XI, King of Castile, surprisingly hated garlic. He founded a knightly order including the rule that any member who ate garlic should not appear in court, or even communicate with other members, for a month! Looking at the history of Spanish cuisine, it is obvious that few of his subjects agreed with him.

In late 14th-century England, there was again evidence of garlic's vulgar connotations. Chaucer's repugnant Summoner, whose face is a mass of bumps and spots, chooses a diet that will heat his blood and sour his breath:

Wel loved he garleek, onions, and eek [also] lekes,
And for to drinken strong wyun, reed as blood.

This is a man of whom "children were aferd."

In the 12th century and later in the 16th century, garlic sauce was a recommended accompaniment to goose, especially if the bird was old and tough.

Changing Fortunes

Shakespeare in the 16th century did not associate garlic with the nobility either. His rough actors in *A Midsummer Night's Dream* are warned by their leader Peter Quince: "And, most dear actors, eat no onions or garlic, for we are to utter sweet breath."

At this time garlic was known as the "poor man's physic." It was reputed to cure many diseases and to ward off countless others, and was probably considered more a medicine than a food. Sailors chewed it because it "pacifyeth the disposition to vomit."

Garlic was going out of culinary favor even in salads, and in the 17th century John Evelyn recommended nothing "beyond a light touch on the dish." From comments in his book *Acetaria*, we can gather that he disapproved of even that much use: "We absolutely forbid it entrance to our Salleting [salad ingredients], by reason of its intolerable Rankness, which made it so detested of old." And again: "The eating of it was (as we read) part of the Punishment for such as had committed the horrid'st Crimes." Where he read it, he does not say, but if it was true, it probably gave the criminals involved a better chance of survival. Other English cookbooks of the 17th century, such as *The Queen's Delight* of 1655, do not refer to garlic.

Eighteenth-century England did not like garlic at all. Neither *The Art of Cookery Made Plain and Easy*, written by Hannah Glasse in 1747, nor *The Experienced English Housekeeper* by Elizabeth Raffald (1782) make any mention of garlic. In *Adam's Luxury and Eve's Cookery*, a gardening and cooking handbook of 1764,

In the 16th century, garlic was considered more as a medicine than a food and was frequently carried on board ships as a good cure for seasickness.

The Spaniard's Garlick Gravy

Slice a pound and a half of Veal, or Beef, pepper or salt it, lay it in a stewpan with a couple of Carrots split, and four cloves of Garlick sliced, a quarter pound of sliced Ham, and a large spoonful of water; – set the stewpan over a gentle fire, and watch when the meat begins to stick to the pan; when it does, turn it, and let it be very well browned (but take care it is not at all burnt); then dredge it with flour, and pour in a quart of broth, a bunch of Sweet Herbs, a couple of cloves bruised, and slice in a Lemon; set it on again, and let it simmer gently for an hour and a half longer; then take off the fat, and strain the gravy from the ingredients, by pouring it through a napkin, straining, and pressing it very hard.

Obs. – *This, it is said, was the secret of the* Old Spaniard, *who kept the House called by that name on* Hampstead Heath.

Those who love Garlick, will find it an extremely rich relish.

The Cook's Oracle: Instituted in the Kitchen of a Physician, 1822

Garlick Sauce

Pound two cloves of Garlick with a piece of fresh Butter about as big as a Nutmeg: rub it through a double hair sieve, and stir it into half a pint of melted butter, or Beef Gravy; or make it with Garlick Vinegar.

The Cook's Oracle: Instituted in the Kitchen of a Physician, 1822

Garlick Vinegar

Garlick is ready for this purpose from Midsummer to Michaelmas.

Peel and chop two ounces of Garlic, pour on them a quart of white-wine Vinegar, stop the jar close, and let it steep ten days, shaking it well every day; then pour off the clear liquor into small bottles.

Obs.—*The cook must be careful not to use too much of this:—a few drops of it will give a pint of gravy a sufficient smack of the Garlick: the flavor of which, when slight, and well blended, is one of the finest we have;—when used in excess, it is the most offensive.*

The best way to use Garlick is to send up some of this Vinegar in a Cruet, and let the company flavor their own Sauce as they like.

The Cook's Oracle: Instituted in the Kitchen of a Physician, 1822

garlic is noted in the growing section but is not included in the calendar of gardening work or in the recipes and culinary directions.

Then, in 1822, came *The Cook's Oracle: Instituted in the Kitchen of a Physician*. A physician would know about medicinal properties of garlic, but this one liked it in the kitchen, too. He makes a Garlick Vinegar by steeping the crushed cloves in wine vinegar, and his "observation" at the end of the recipe says:

> *The cook must be careful not to use too much of this:- a few drops of it will give a pint of gravy a sufficient smack of the Garlick: the flavor of which, when slight, and well blended, is one of the finest we have:- when used in excess, it is the most offensive.*

He goes on: "The best way to use Garlic is to send up some of this Vinegar in a Cruet, and let the company flavor their own Sauce as they like." Our cook-physician has a recipe for Garlic Sauce as well, made by mixing two crushed cloves (or a little of his Garlick Vinegar) with a melted knob of butter and some beef gravy. Then there is The Spaniard's Garlick Gravy, made by stewing veal or beef with slices of ham, carrots, and four sliced garlic cloves. Toward the end of the cooking time, he puts in flour, herbs, cloves, and a slice of lemon, simmers everything a bit longer and strains off the liquid. Again there is an observation: "This, it is said, was the secret of the Old Spaniard, who kept the House called by that name on Hampstead Heath. Those who love Garlick will find it an extremely rich relish."

The physician was a true fan of garlic, but what about other 19th-century English cooks? Eliza Acton's *Modern Cookery for Private Families* appeared in 1845. In more than 600

"The smell of this plant is generally considered offensive, and it is the most acrimonious in its taste of the whole of the alliaceous tribe. In 1548 it was introduced to England from the shores of the Mediterranean, where it is abundant, and in Sicily it grows naturally. It was in greater repute with our ancestors than it is with ourselves, although it is still used as a seasoning herb. In Europe, especially in Italy, it is much used, and the French consider it is an essential in many made dishes."

MRS. BEETON, 1861

pages there are only three mentions of garlic, so she hardly considered it an important ingredient. But she was not disparaging of it either. She makes a Garlic Vinegar very similar in method and eventual use to the cook-physician's, and a Bengal Chutney in which crab apples, sour apples, unripe bullaces (wild plums), and garlic are the main ingredients.

Mrs. Acton's main garlic recipe is for Mild Ragoût of Garlic in which garlic cloves (the number is not stated) are treated more like a vegetable than a flavoring ingredient. They are peeled, boiled in several changes of salted water—for about 20 minutes each time—until they are tender, and then either served plainly with roast mutton or "put into good brown gravy or white sauce for the table." One wonders just how much flavor was left, for Mrs. Acton says: "By changing very frequently the water in which it is boiled, the root will be deprived of its naturally pungent flavor and smell, and rendered extremely mild: when it is not wished to be quite so much so, change the water every ten minutes only."

Then in 1861 came Mrs. Beeton, the person who probably did most to influence English cooking at the time, and she thoroughly disliked garlic, considering its smell "offensive." Did she, with one stroke of her pen, put every English housewife off garlic for the next hundred years? It could well be so. She uses garlic in just one recipe, for Bengal Chutney, which is not her own but was given to her by a friend "who had long been resident in India."

In the United States, Fannie Farmer was writing her *Original Boston Cooking School Cookbook* which came out in 1896, and that has

In present-day France, just as in the past, the itinerant garlic seller is always a welcome sight to lovers of good food.

"An edible plant whose bulbs are used for seasoning. It has an acrid, volatile juice that makes the eyes water. Applied to the skin, it reddens and even burns it . . ."

"Everybody knows the odor of garlic except the one who has eaten it and wonders why everybody turns away from him . . ."

ALEXANDRE DUMAS, *LE GRAND DICTIONNAIRE DE CUISINE*, 1873

Bunches of garlic, hung in a cool, airy place, will keep fresh for several months. They are also an attractive decoration.

Garlic is available in many different forms. Garlic-flavored pasta and potato chips are just two of the many garlic products on sale.

no mention of garlic at all. But Fannie might be excused, as she lived and worked on the northeast coast. Away down in the south and west, cooking was being influenced by Mexican styles and by the foods of former African slaves, all of which contained garlic. So, although not brought by the northern European settlers, garlic was creeping into North America through another door.

In France and southern Europe, garlic had never fallen from grace. It was still adored as a flavoring ingredient and respected as a curer of ills. Alexandre Dumas, he who recounted the story of the Roman Horace, reflected the French attitude when he wrote in his *Le Grand Dictionnaire de Cuisine* (1873): "Provençal cooking is based on garlic. The air is saturated with garlic, which makes it very healthful."

So, what of the past hundred years? The cultures which have remained unchanged in their loyalty to the bulb are numerous. They include those of southern Europe, the Middle East, India, Asia, Southeast Asia, China, Central and South America, and the southern United States.

In Britain, Mrs. Beeton's attitude long prevailed, and in country kitchens garlic had no place. A good indicator of this was a book called *Farmhouse Fare*, published in 1946, and including recipes sent in by readers of *Farmer's Weekly*. Search through the whole book and you will find no mention of garlic, not even in

Garlic is sold alongside vegetables and herbs in markets all over the world. These garlic stalls are in Paris (right) and Singapore's China Town (below).

Although garlic can easily be grown in a garden or flowerpot, most people buy the commercially grown product. It is usually harvested in mid to late summer.

chutneys and sauces. Dorothy Hartley wrote a wonderful appreciation of English food in 1954 which she called *Food in England*. There is no *Allium sativum*, but there is wild garlic whose "white lacy flowers, plucked in shady woods, make a savory garnish to the spring salad."

The Resurgence of Garlic

Yet, as we saw at the beginning of the chapter, garlic can now be bought in practically every country; garlic bread, garlic cheese and garlic rice are just a few of the garlic-flavored products on supermarket shelves everywhere. People are also beginning to rediscover the plant's wonderful health-giving properties. Why did the fortunes of garlic turn, yet again, to place it among our most valuable ingredients?

Garlic and fresh herbs are important flavoring ingredients worldwide, and provide a feast for the eye as well as the stomach!

One answer is that the world has become "smaller" as transport has become faster and cheaper. In the late 1950s, people started to travel. Conservative northerners visited the exotic south and discovered the colorful cuisine of sunnier climes with its vegetables, rice, pasta, oil, herbs, and garlic. They liked what they found and looked for it back home.

At the same time, others had journeyed in the opposite direction. To Britain came people from Africa, the Caribbean and Asia, to settle and become naturalized but all longing for a taste of their traditional home-cooking. British farmers could not be persuaded to change their crops overnight, and traditional importers were unwilling to ship exotic goods that might not sell. The new British, therefore, decided to do it for themselves. They became importers, storekeepers, and market traders, buying and selling foods such as okra, garlic, and yams, previously never set alongside the home-grown cabbages, carrots, and parsley. Their food was enticing, their ways of cooking it delicious—and gradually the habit spread.

Then came a new generation of cookbooks, influenced at first by writers such as Elizabeth David, but later borne on a wave of their own cooking, which introduced new flavors and new methods. People have also become interested in the health-giving properties of food. We have learned what we should have remembered all along, that "you are what you eat," and the quality, type, and balance of your diet can affect your well-being. Vegetarian food has became popular and so have ways of flavoring without too much salt.

Today's climate creates the ideal conditions for an ingredient like garlic to thrive. New foods, new recipes, a new perspective on health, a mixing of cultures, and new enthusiams all helped to bring it back into favor, from which it seems unlikely to fall.

A marinade of wine and garlic and a thick topping of rosemary leaves will always enhance barbecued lamb. Garlic has been both appreciated and reviled during its long history but luckily has survived all onslaughts to become a firm culinary favorite.

The Main Types *of* Garlic

Garlic is a member of the lily family and a close relative of onions, leeks, scallions, and chives. It is a perennial plant, which means, left in the ground, it will grow and flower every spring and summer without having to be resown or replanted.

The garlic plant grows from the center of a round, slightly irregular-shaped bulb. The size of the bulb differs according to the variety and the growing conditions, as do its flavor, color, and quality. It can be as tall as it is wide, or it may be somewhat compressed from top to bottom. The base of the bulb is slightly flattened and the top, from which the leaf and flower stems will emerge, is pointed. Underneath the first layers of papery skin, the bulb is composed of around 10 crescent-shaped cloves, each wrapped in its own layers of thin skin. Once the bulb has been harvested, drying ensures the cloves are easy to pull apart and the bulb is long-lasting. Garlic leaves are flat and gray-green, and the small, lily-like flowers grow on a single stem in a round head. Their most usual color is pink-white. Sometimes tiny bulbs (bulbils) grow among the flowers; these can be picked and used fresh.

Common Garlic (Allium sativum)

This is grown both domestically and commercially. It is the most common form of garlic, with the finest flavor and the best properties. There are many cultivated varieties within this group. The skins can be white, creamy yellow, red or purple, and the color of the cloves may echo that of the skin. The leaves can measure from 12 inches to 24 inches in height and the flowers can vary in color from white through pink to purple and blue.

In the United States, the white-skinned types of garlic are generally referred to as American or Californian garlic, and of these there are early and late varieties. South Australian White is also grown in the U.S.A. Mexican garlic, which is harvested early, in April and May, and imported into California, is a creamy purple color. Other purple-skinned bulbs are Italian Purple, Chilean, and Creole garlic. Large-cloved varieties include Giant Russian, New Zealand Purple, and Glenlarge.

Green Garlic

Green garlic is ordinary *Allium sativum* which has been harvested between March and May before the cloves have developed and when the flavor is very delicate and fresh. The green garlic plant is rather like a scallion, with a small, bulbous end and a green stalk. All parts of the plant can be used. The green parts make an ideal salad herb and the mild-flavored bulb can be used in cooked dishes where only a gentle garlic flavor is required.

Was Garlic the Emblem of Wales?

In her book Food in England *(1954), Dorothy Hartley says of wild garlic: "Wild garlic grows to such an extent in parts of Wales that we believe it to have been the origin of the national emblem [leeks]."*

Elephant Garlic (Allium ampeloprasum *and* Allium gigantum)

Both types, when growing, look more like leeks than garlic, with a profusion of leaves. The bulbs reach the size of a large orange and are divided into only four to six cloves. *A. ampeloprasum*, also known as *d'orient* (oriental garlic), grows up to 3 feet high and has pink to pale green flowers. *A. gigantum* can grow even taller. It has wider leaves and pale lilac flowers. The flavor of elephant garlic does not match its size. It is very mild, with no pungency, and becomes even blander when it is cooked. It does, however, make a good salad ingredient for those who like the flavor of garlic to remain in the background.

Garlic Chives (Allium tuberosum)

These grow like chives and have hardy, flat leaves. They have a pleasant, mild garlic flavor, which makes them an ideal salad herb.

Ramsons (Allium ursinum)

Ramsons are the wild garlic of the damp woods of Britain and continental Europe, also called broad-leaved garlic. They have leaves like those of lily of the valley, and heads of starry, white flowers. Although they used to be a favorite "pot-herb" in peasant dishes, ramsons have a distinctive acrid flavor and smell.

Rocambole (Allium sativum *'ophioscorodon'*)

This is also called Italian, French, Serpent, or Top-setting garlic and is actually a native of Denmark, where it was once used for flavoring cheese. Its leaves are flat and profuse, and its flower heads grow in loops which make them look like snakes with pointed heads (its name is derived from the Greek word *ophis*, meaning snake). When the heads open they reveal bulbils that, like the rest of the plant, are edible. The bulbs are harvested in the same way as those of *A. sativum*; they keep well and have a good flavor.

Crow Garlic (Allium vineale)

This is another wild garlic that was once common in Britain and Europe. It grew in damp pastures, and when eaten by cows it gave a rather unpleasant taste to milk and butter. It has small bulbs and, like ramsons, an acrid flavor.

Growing Garlic

Garlic is one of the easiest of herbs to cultivate. You can grow it in a garden plot, in a tub, or even in a flower pot. It is also grown commercially on a large scale.

In the agricultural year, every activity has its allotted month. Garlic can be planted at the time of the grain harvest and also at the time of plowing.

Garlic is not propagated from seed, but from the cloves. You can buy garlic for planting from a specialist plant supplier or your usual grocery store. The garlic that you buy for cooking is perfectly adequate for cultivation. Choose healthy specimens with large cloves that are not shriveled or beginning to sprout. There should not be any soft spots, mildew, or discoloration, and you should be able to separate the cloves easily without damaging them.

When to Plant

In temperate climates—such as those of most of northern Europe—where the ground does not freeze solid for long periods during the winter, garlic can be planted in the fall, about four weeks before the first hard frosts. This would be in September or early October, and a little later in warmer climates.

Fall-sown garlic has a longer growing time and therefore tends to be bigger than garlic sown in the spring. However, lengthy periods in frozen soil could rot the cloves and where harsh conditions prevail it is better to plant in the spring. Spring-planted garlic does not lag too far behind once the warmer weather begins. To allow a good, long growing period, plant cloves in early March.

Preparation of Garlic for Planting

If you are planting in a climate where the winter temperature drops below 50°F, the garlic cloves need no preparation. However, you could follow the advice of some of the older gardening writers, who recommended dressing

Medieval Lore

If garlic is both planted and harvested when the moon is below the horizon, its pungency will be far less.

This illustration, from a 15th-century French calendar and Book of Hours, *shows a farmer sowing his crop. Cloves of garlic must be planted separately, about 2 inches deep.*

the cloves with wood-ash or soot to repel insects, prevent disease, and make the soil slightly alkaline, which garlic likes.

If your winter climate stays above that temperature, it is advisable to chill the garlic cloves before planting. This stimulates growth to an even-sized bulb and ensures that the skins will be sufficiently thick for good storage. Separate the cloves, keep them at a temperature of 50°F for one month and plant them when the ground is at its coolest.

Preparation of the Soil and Planting

Ideally garlic needs a sunny spot in a light, sandy, well-drained soil enriched with manure or compost. It can be planted in the vegetable patch, in the herb garden, or among flowers.

Rake over the soil and, using a dibber, make holes 2 inches deep and 8 inches apart, allowing 12 inches between the rows. This gives you room for hoeing and weeding later. Put the garlic cloves into the holes, with the sprouting end uppermost. Cover them over and firm the soil with the back of a rake.

Care after Planting

In dry weather, water the garlic regularly. As soon as the tops sprout, begin clearing the weeds around them regularly to prevent the plants from being choked. Mulching the ground around the plants will control weeds and keep the soil cool. Use compost, last fall's leaves, or mulches such as lucerne or clover-hay. Leave the mulch on the top of the soil. If it is dug in, it may encourage pests.

Flowers

Fall-sown garlic will flower in the late spring or early summer. The flowers can be picked and used in salads. The bulbils that appear among the flowers should be removed to encourage the growth of the main bulb. They also make a good salad ingredient. Some gardening writers recommend the flower stem should be bent over as it forms, to ensure the good growth of the bulb.

Growing Garlic in Tubs

Garlic can be grown in garden tubs with great success. Make sure that the tubs are in a sunny spot and are filled with light but enriched soil. Plant the cloves, in fall or spring, allowing a clear radius of 4 inches around each one. Keep them well watered and well drained.

Planting in the 18th Century

Garlic

This is increased by the Roots, which will part into small cloves, each of which are to be planted separately in a Bed of tolerable good Earth, in February or March, at about five inches apart every way; and when they are grown pretty high we generally tie the In-tops on a Knot, which prevents their spindling, and causes the Root to be larger. In July or August, when their In-leaves turn yellow, they must be digged up and spread abroad in the Sun and dried; and so cutting off the small Fibers and part of the Top, tie them up in Bunches and hang them up for use.

Adam's Luxury and Eve's Cookery, Anonymous, 1764

Elephant garlic (Allium gigantum) *in flower. When garlic bulbs are left in the ground, they produce beautiful round heads of flowers the following spring.*

Growing Garlic in a Flowerpot

In fall, fill a 6-inch diameter flowerpot with potting compost. Plant a single garlic clove about 1 inch deep. Put the pot in a cool, dark cupboard and keep the compost moist. When the plant begins to sprout (around December), transfer the pot to a cool room or conservatory. In March, put the pot outside. The garlic should flower in the usual way, and the bulb can be harvested in August.

Companion Planting

Garlic is rich in sulfur and is generally considered to be beneficial to the soil. The substances released from its roots are thought to encourage the growth of neighboring plants. Roses particularly benefit from having garlic planted near them, and garlic is said to increase their scent. Garlic grown under peach trees is reputed to cure leaf curl. Peas and beans, however, do not benefit from having garlic grown near them.

Harvesting

Garlic should be harvested when the leaves are beginning to look leathery and dry. Fall-planted garlic is usually ready in July, and spring-planted garlic in August, but this may vary according to the summer weather. If the summer has been cool and damp, garlic may not be ready for harvesting until September. Choose a sunny, dry day. Loosen the soil around and under the garlic with a fork so you can take hold of the leaves and gently pull the bulb from the ground leaving the whole plant intact. An alternative method is to lift the bulb out of the ground from underneath with a long trowel. The roots are usually insignificant and can be "rubbed off" easily. Then lay the bulbs on the earth in the sun and leave them for about two hours.

Garlic is very easy to cultivate and can be grown in the garden or even in a flowerpot.

Commercial Garlic Growing in California

Several cultivated varieties of Allium sativum *are grown in the Californian garlic fields, and most of the harvesting is done in July. One acre yields about 1,300 pounds of garlic bulbs.*

After being pulled out of the ground, the plants are left to dry in the sun, arranged in rows and facing into the prevailing wind, with the foliage of one plant covering the bulb of the next to prevent sun-scald. Straw or dirt may also be used to cover the drying bulbs. This process is known as curing, and it takes about three weeks, depending on the size of the plants and on the weather. Once the garlic is cured, it is trimmed by hand, graded and sorted, and sent to market.

Buying and Storing Garlic

When buying garlic, look for large, clean, firm bulbs with dry, unbroken skins.

Store bulbs and individual cloves in a special garlic pot, a wire basket, or a mesh bag. The bulbs can also be kept on a vegetable rack. Always place the garlic in a cool, airy place, away from steam. Do not put it in the refrigerator where the temperature spoils its flavor and dries it.

Garlic will keep for up to two months in ideal conditions.

Bulbs of garlic with the dried stems twisted into a braid make an attractive decoration. Keep them in a dry atmosphere.

In warm, dry climates, garlic can be left out in the sun and wind to dry. Here, the untrimmed bulbs have been spread out on racks so they will dry evenly.

DRYING

Gently rub as much dirt from the bulbs and the roots as you can, and then pull away the grubby outer layer of skin. Do not remove the tops.

Spread some racks or several thicknesses of old newspaper in a dry, airy shed and arrange the garlic bulbs on them. Leave them for about a week or until the leaves are completely dry.

STORING

Garlic is ready for storing when the skin becomes dry and papery and when the root crown is hard. To store, braid the bulbs together, or tie them in bunches. Alternatively, remove the tops and put the bulbs into a net bag. Hang the garlic up in a cool, dry place.

The garlic is now ready for use; remove one bulb at a time, as required. Home-grown bulbs should keep for about six months, provided they do not become excessively cold or damp.

If your garlic becomes soft and moldy or hard and shriveled, or if it starts to sprout, this will harm the flavor. Garlic should never be frozen as this alters the flavor completely.

SAVING CLOVES FOR NEXT YEAR

To obtain the same-sized crop next year, you need to save about 10 percent of your cloves. Choose cloves from the biggest heads of garlic and store them in a cool, dry place until required for planting.

PERENNIAL GARLIC

If you have a suitable patch of ground, you can leave garlic in the soil instead of harvesting it. The bulbs will gradually spread underground, and you will have green garlic for salads every year. If the patch of perennial garlic becomes too large, you can always dig up selected bulbs in the fall.

Garlic and other herbs were "cried" in city streets from medieval times until the beginning of the 20th century. This engraving from 1909 shows a garlic and bay seller.

Yesterday's Cure-all

A preventer of disease, a giver of strength, a cure for such diverse complaints as whooping cough, worms, constipation, and dropsy: there is hardly an ailment for which garlic has not been prescribed at some time in history.

One of the vernacular names for garlic is Poor Man's Treacle, not a description of the flavor, but from the word *theriac*, a Latin term meaning "cure-all." Because of its easy cultivation and prolific growth, garlic has always been readily accessible to ordinary people, who for thousands of years have taken advantage of its many health-giving properties.

The 5,000-year-old Ayurvedic method of healing—a form of herbal medicine used in India—always included garlic in its treatments, particularly for digestive disorders, hoarseness, and typhus, and these cures are still practiced. Similarly, garlic has been prescribed in Chinese medicine for the past 4,000 years.

The ancient Egyptians drew up medical texts on papyri. One of these, the *Book of the Dead*, lists 22 garlic remedies, including those for worms and heart problems. Although one Egyptian treatment for worms was to hang a string of garlic around the sufferer's neck rather than using the plant as an internal remedy, most of the cures are based on sound scientific facts and are still relevant today. Garlic was applied to insect and snake bites, and placing garlic bulbs around the house was thought to keep serpents and scorpions away.

In Egypt, and in many other civilisations, garlic was not only a cure but a preventative, given to fortify workers and to protect them from epidemics and water-borne diseases. The ancient Greeks and Romans recognized the properties of the plant as a disease preventer and general tonic. Hippocrates, who is known as the "father of medicine," based some of his ideas on Egyptian methods, and prescribed garlic treatments, including using it as a diuretic and as a laxative. In his treatise *On Sterile Women*, he recommends the following:

Take a clove of garlic, clean it, remove the skin and insert as a pessary, and the following morning discover whether the woman's breath smells of garlic; if it does, she will conceive; if not, she will not.

This was really only a general indication of the patient's health, based on the principle that garlic oil, once absorbed by the body, is always excreted through the lungs and can therefore be smelled on the breath. If this was so for the

In ancient Egypt, garlic was thought to be both a protection against and a cure for snake bites and is listed as such in the 21st-Dynasty Book of the Dead.

Many snakes are extremely venomous and well deserve their deadly reputation. If the ancient writings are to be believed, garlic could keep them away from your camp or house.

woman in question it showed that her system was in good working order and the physicians could draw the conclusion that she would be fit for childbearing.

Dioscorides, a Roman physician, used a mixture of milk, garlic, and honey as a remedy for hoarseness and a sore throat. He recognized the tonic properties of garlic, and also prescribed it for asthma and worms, and as a diuretic. He even had a cure for mouse bites using a plaster made from garlic, fig leaves, and cumin. Another garlic plaster was used for the relief of hemorrhoids.

The Roman poet Virgil, in a poem called "The Passionate Shepherd to his Love," described the use of garlic as a general

In 1664, during the Great Plague, everyone wanted garlic to keep the infection away and, weight for weight, garlic bulbs became more valuable than gold.

restorative for laborers on the land. There was, he says, "a fragrant soup of pounded garlic and wild-thyme for the reapers wearied by the scorching heat."

Like the Egyptians, the Romans used garlic to ward off snakes and scorpions. The writer Pliny included this application in his *Historia Naturalis*, along with 60 other garlic remedies for conditions as diverse as madness, coughs, wild animal bites, and low libido. To prepare garlic for medicinal use, he said, it should be crushed and boiled in honey with wine or coriander.

Many Roman cures lasted into medieval times. The use of garlic for bites and stings—also recommended by the prophet Mohammed—was advised by the English scholar Alexander Neckam as late as the 12th century. The Anglo-Saxons knew garlic well, and simmered it in "hen broth" as a cure for constipation.

Enormous amounts of garlic were grown in monastery gardens all over medieval Europe. The harvested bulbs were braided together, hung up to dry, and then used as an antiseptic dressing for wounds or pounded into goose grease as a remedy for chest complaints. Garlic was also added to food to prevent infections from spreading within the closed confines of the monastery.

Doctors in Venice during an outbreak of plague in the 17th century wore grotesque masks to keep infection at bay – eating garlic proved more successful.

Garlic - Allium ampeloprasum

DESCRIPTION—The root consists of several cloves, or small bulbs of a reddish white color, set together in a round compass, and enclosed in a common skinny coat or cover, having several small fibers at the bottom; the leaves are broad and long, like those of leeks; on top of the stalk, which grows two or three feet high, stands an umbel of small white five-leaved flowers. The whole plant, especially the root, is of a very strong and offensive smell.

PLACE—It is a native of the East, but for its use is cultivated everywhere in gardens.

TIME—It flowers in June and July.

GOVERNMENT AND VIRTUES—Mars owns this herb. This was anciently accounted the poor man's treacle, it being a remedy for all diseases and hurts (except those which itself breeds). It provokes urine and women's courses, helps the biting of mad dogs, and other venomous creatures; kills the worms in children, cuts and voids tough phlegm, purges the head, helps the lethargy, is a good preservative against, and a remedy for, any plague, sore, or for ulcer; takes away spots and blemishes in the skin, eases pains in the ears, ripens and breaks imposthumes, or other swellings; and for all diseases the onions are as effectual. But the Garlic has some more peculiar virtues besides the former, viz. it has a special quality to discuss inconveniences, coming by corrupt agues or mineral vapors, or by drinking corrupt and stinking waters; as also by taking wolf-bane, hen-bane, hemlock, or other poisonous and dangerous herbs. It is also held good in hydropic diseases, the jaundice, falling sickness, cramps, convulsions, the piles or hemorrhoides, or other cold diseases. Authors quote many other diseases this is good for; but conceal its vices. Its heat is very vehement; and all vehement hot things send up but ill savors to the brain. In choleric men it will add fuel to the fire; in men oppressed by melancholy, it will attenuate the humor, and send up strong fancies, and as many strange visions to the head; therefore let it be taken inwardly with great moderation; outwardly, you may make more bold with it.

NICHOLAS CULPEPER, *THE ENGLISH PHYSICIAN*, *c.*1640

Nicholas Culpeper (top) trained as an apothecary in the 17th century. His book The English Physician *(above) was intended for home use by ordinary people and was extremely popular during his lifetime and for long afterward. The edition shown here was published in 1814.*

The monks were often responsible for treating the sick who lived in their area and also wandering beggars, including lepers, who knocked at the monastery gates. Garlic was one of the accepted treatments for leprosy, giving lepers the name of "pilgarlics," because they had to peel their own cloves. Monks and medieval doctors going out into the community in times of plague often wore masks stuffed with garlic to ward off infection.

In medieval France and England, garlic was chewed by farm laborers to maintain their strength and resistance to disease, and was carried by pilgrims to keep them healthy on their journey. It was also one of the green herbs put into pottages, the thick soups which were the staple of the medieval diet for ordinary people and eaten as an antidote to scurvy.

In the 16th century, garlic maintained its reputation among the poor, though its smell had made it less popular with the gentry, even for curative purposes. In his *Book of Simples* (1562), William Bullein said that garlic was a gross kind of medicine, very unpleasant for "fayre Ladyes" who "preferre sweete breathes before gentle wordes." John Gerard, who wrote a very detailed herbal in 1597, made no mention of garlic.

In 1608, when an epidemic of plague hit London, the upper classes would neither eat nor use garlic, not even the priests who went out regularly to administer to the sick and dying. Garlic-eating French priests apparently survived the work, whereas many, perhaps more genteel, English priests died.

Nicolas Culpeper, the 17th-century herbalist, listed countless uses for garlic even though he comments on the "very strong and offensive smell." He says it is "a remedy for all diseases and hurts (except those which itself breeds)." Among his treatments are cures for bites, worms, cuts, head colds and chest complaints, boils, poison, jaundice, and cramp. On the down side, "in men oppressed by melancholy, it will attenuate the humor, and send up strong fancies, and as many strange visions to the head; therefore let it be taken inwardly with great moderation; outwardly, you may make more bold with it."

In 17th-century England, country people continued to use garlic fairly widely as a remedy. In her book *The Compleat Cook: The Secrets of a Seventeenth Century Housewife*, Rebecca Price gives two medicinal recipes for garlic—one for a syrup and one for preserved garlic—both recommended for coughs, colds, and consumption. Many writers of the time advised infusing or boiling garlic before taking it so as to diminish the odor.

When plague was raging in Marseilles, in southern France, in 1720, four notorious robbers broke into the houses of the dead and dying, stealing their clothes and valuables. The pillagers survived hale and hearty, thanks to drinking their concoction of garlic macerated in red wine, which became known as the Vinegar of the Four Thieves.

Around the Mediterranean, in the 18th and 19th centuries, garlic was used to prevent sunburn and sunstroke, as it had been in Roman times. Workers in the fields ate it and also rubbed it on their lips and noses before going out into the sun.

Garlic's antiseptic properties had been so well established by the beginning of the 20th century that, during World War I, it was used in field hospitals to prevent septic poisoning and gangrene. The garlic was crushed, and the juice expressed, mixed with water, and put on swabs of sphagnum moss, which were then applied to the wound. In 1916, the British government offered everyone in the country one shilling (5p) per pound for as many bulbs as they could produce to keep the hospitals supplied. Writing of the garlic swab treatment in *A Modern Herbal* (1931), Mrs. M. Grieve maintained that "thousands of men have been saved by its use."

After World War I, garlic was used by the Russians as a cheap and effective cure, and became known as Russian penicillin. It was employed again by the Russians, and also the British and Germans, during World War II.

Throughout the first half of the 20th century, garlic continued to be a well-known country cure, even though in countries such as Britain it all but disappeared from the dining table. Children had their chests rubbed with goose grease and garlic, or simply with a cut clove, to ease coughs, colds and whooping cough. The same mixture rubbed into limbs and joints relieved rheumatism and arthritis. Eating it regularly was said to cure epilepsy, a cut clove was a country woman's smelling salts, and garlic macerated in wine was recognized as a good digestive. The gypsies, who have always used it, revere its powers and call it moly.

To find a name for me the gods took care
A mystic name that might my worth declare
They call me moly

ANCIENT ROMANY VERSE

In the past, a plentiful supply of garlic meant good health for all the family. Garlic's reputation as a healthy ingredient is now firmly established and it is found in nearly all pharmacies and supermarkets.

Today's Medicine

For thousands of years garlic has been an easily accessible remedy for ordinary people, and over the last thirty years scientific research has proved many of the old claims for it to be true.

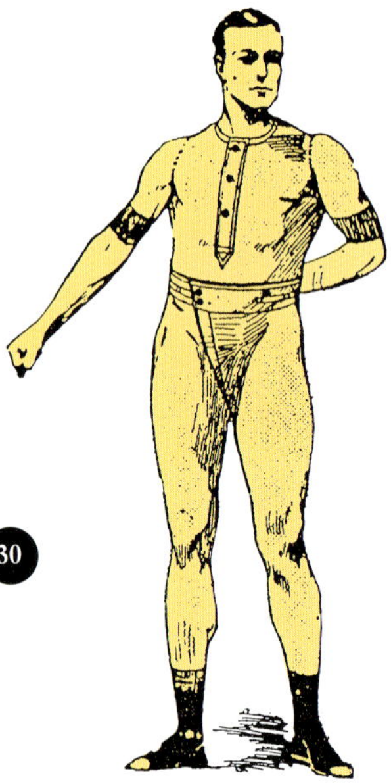

Garlic is now medically proven to be a valuable aid to maintaining good health, confirming its long-held reputation.

During the 1980s and 1990s researchers in Germany, India, Japan, the United States, and elsewhere have been looking into the possible uses of garlic as a means of reducing blood cholesterol, and also high blood pressure, as a control for blood clotting, and as a potential aid in the treatment of some forms of cancer. The first World Congress on the Significance of Garlic and Garlic Constituents was held in Washington, D.C. in 1990.

Although some aspects of the action of garlic and what it can cure remain unclear, the emerging picture confirms many of its historical medicinal uses. Most researchers agree that a regular intake of garlic is beneficial to all-round health. Garlic is a true food remedy—an example of how plants are frequently food and medicine combined.

All the constituents of garlic are beneficial. It has vitamins A and B; it is rich in alkaline salts and sulfur-containing amino acids; and, above all, it holds significant amounts of a highly volatile oil. This oil includes a substance called alliin, which, as soon as the cloves are cut or crushed, is converted to allicin. After a short exposure to the air, the allicin is in turn converted to diallydisulphide. It is this last substance which gives garlic its antibacterial effect.

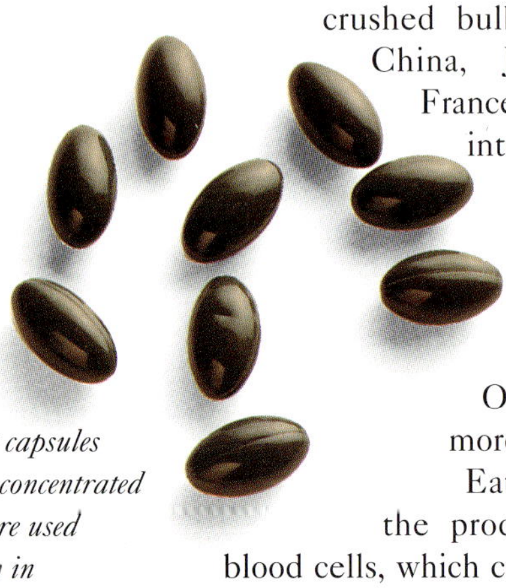

Garlic capsules containing concentrated garlic oil are used medicinally in many countries.

Garlic oil extracted by steam from the crushed bulb is used medicinally in China, Japan, Egypt, Bulgaria, France, and Germany. It is made into garlic capsules and put into health-food products. Some medical writers claim that garlic taken in this form is just as good as the raw clove. Others state that raw garlic is more effective.

Eaten regularly, garlic can aid the production of healthy white blood cells, which combat infection, and it can help to destroy bacteria which attack the body. This same antibacterial effect aids digestion. Garlic can encourage beneficial bacterial to form in the digestive tract, while simultaneously killing unwanted ones. Garlic also whets the appetite, encouraging you to eat if you have lost your desire for food. Regular consumption can help to combat flatulence.

Once taken into the body, the volatile oil of garlic is excreted through the lungs without having lost any of its beneficial properties. That is how it can be useful in treating infections of the respiratory tract, such as coughs and the common cold.

Garlic has long been thought to be good for the blood. Its alkaline salts and sulfur components act as blood purifiers. Raw garlic is effective in lowering blood pressure and so it can minimise the risk of a stroke. It can also reduce the fatty deposits that build up in the walls of arteries causing arteriosclerosis (heart disease). Recent research has found that garlic reduces LDL cholesterol (low-density lipoprotein cholesterol—the type we do not want) and increases HDL cholesterol (high-density—the type that is beneficial).

Garlic is a vermifuge, that is, it can help to rid the body of parasites. As well as unwanted intestinal "guests," such as worms, there are also various skin disorders which can be cured by garlic, particularly those where the skin has been infected by microorganisms. Ringworm is an example, where the skin is infected by a fungus. Impetigo, a highly contagious condition easily picked up by children, can be alleviated by a diet rich in vitamin-C containing vegetables and garlic.

If you suffer from warts, garlic eaten regularly can cleanse the lymphatic system and therefore help to get rid of them. Garlic is also a natural antiseptic and squeezing a little juice onto minor wounds will assist them to heal quickly and cleanly. Research has found that injections of garlic extract helped to cure tumors in rats, so garlic might in the future be recommended as part of a diet to combat the effects of cancer.

GARLIC CURES

As a preventive and general tonic, an aid to good digestion, and a means of maintaining optimum blood pressure, garlic should be eaten regularly, at least once a day. The simplest way to do this is to crush it and put it into a salad dressing, such as the one on page 115. Here are some other simple remedies to try for minor complaints and ailments. If you are in any doubt about your health you should contact a doctor or a medicinal herbalist.

Gargle for a Sore Throat

Put 1¼ cups water into a saucepan. Add 1 slice fresh ginger root, pinch cayenne pepper, 1 garlic clove (cut in half), 1tsp cider vinegar, and 2tsp honey. Bring everything to a boil, then remove from the heat, cover and leave until cool. Strain the liquid and use it as a gargle three times a day.

Syrup of Garlic for Coughs and Colds

Put 1¼ cups cider vinegar into a saucepan. Add 1tbsp caraway seeds and 1tbsp fennel seeds. Bring to a boil, add 4tbsp chopped garlic and simmer for 5 minutes. Strain. Return the liquid to the cleaned pan and add ¾ cup honey. Bring to a boil again and boil hard for 5 minutes. Allow the syrup to cool and transfer it to a jar. For adults, take 1tbsp every two hours. Reduce the dosage to 1tsp for children.

To Ease a Chest Infection

Rub the soles of your feet with a cut garlic clove. The garlic's natural oil will be absorbed through your skin and carried by the blood to the lungs. Rub your chest with garlic oil, made as for rheumatism.

Garlic Oil for Rheumatism and Sprains

Put 1 cup good-quality oil, such as olive or wheat-germ oil, into a bottle. Peel and crush 4 cloves of garlic and add them to the oil. Cover tightly and leave the bottle in a warm place for 7 days. Strain off the oil and put it into a clean bottle. Use as an embrocation, rubbing a little on to the affected part every day.

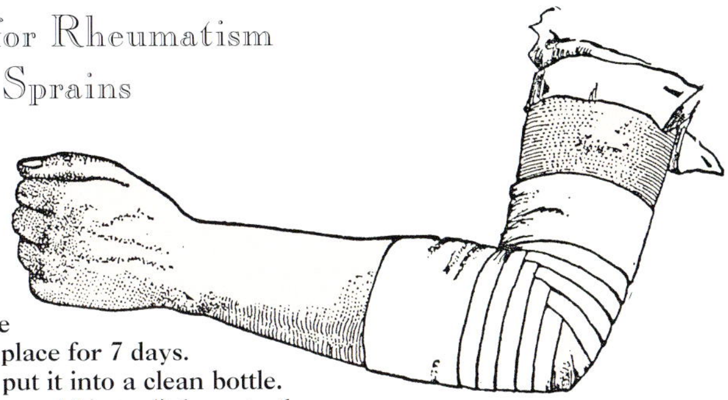

Infusion for Colds and Chest Complaints

Crush 2oz garlic cloves and put them into a jug. Pour on 1 cup boiling water, cover, and leave for 12 hours. Strain off the liquid. For adults, take 1tbsp every two hours. For children, reduce the amount of garlic and the dosage as follows:

1 to 5 years	*1oz garlic; 1 teaspoon*
5 to 12 years	*1½oz garlic; 2 teaspoons*

Remedy for an Ant or Mosquito Bite

Rub the bite with a cut clove of garlic.

To Relieve a Head Cold

Several times a day, inhale the oil from a cut or crushed garlic clove.

Remedy for Corns

Cut a sliver of garlic the same size as the corn. Put it on top of the corn and hold it in place with a bandage. Replace the garlic sliver every day until the corn drops off.

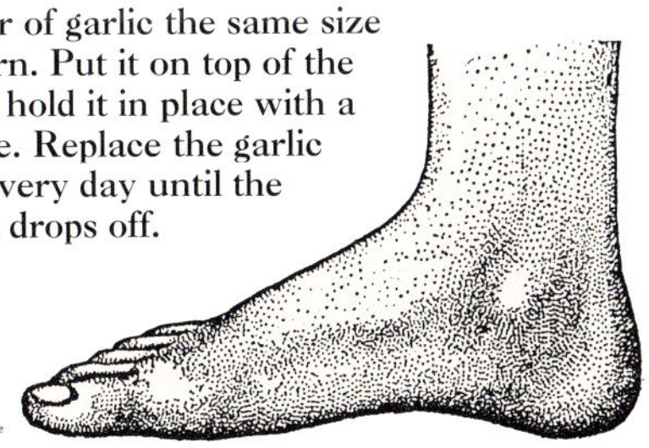

THE LORE *and* LEGEND *of* GARLIC

THE STRONG ODOR AND REMARKABLE MEDICINAL PROPERTIES OF GARLIC HAVE, OVER THE CENTURIES, CAUSED IT TO BE ENDOWED WITH MANY MAGICAL QUALITIES. IT HAS BEEN ACCORDED POWERS OF HEALING, PROTECTION, AND EXORCISM; IT HAS BEEN USED TO PROMOTE LUST AND DETER THEFT; IT HAS EVEN BEEN REGARDED AS SACRED.

In ancient Greece, offerings of garlic were made to the goddess Hecate, here seen in her triple form of maiden, mother, and crone, and garlic was often referred to as "Hecate's supper."

According to Pliny, garlic was so greatly revered by the ancient Egyptians that they believed it to be divine and called upon it when swearing an oath. The Roman satirist Juvenal said, "Each clove of garlic hath a sacred flower," and European gypsies considered garlic, or "moly," as they called it, to be sacred.

In classical mythology, garlic was a masculine plant, ruled by Mars, the god of war and the element of fire. It was also sacred to Hecate, the dark goddess of the night sky, the underworld and enchantment. The protector of flocks, sailors, and wise women, she was also said to haunt graveyards and the scenes of crimes as the goddess of purification and expiation, qualities which have also been linked to garlic.

Statues of Hecate frequently depicted her in the triple form of maiden, mother, and crone, and were sited at crossroads—places where the traveler faced three choices of direction. Ancient Greeks who wished to make her an offering would bring garlic, which was often referred to as "Hecate's supper." It had to be given in the middle of the night, on the eve of the full moon. The offerer set the garlic on a pile of stones provided for the purpose and had to walk away quickly without looking back. The earliest description we have of these offerings to Hecate was written by Theophrastus in 4 to 3 B.C.

The belief that garlic can protect from harm has been shared by many civilisations. It has the reputation of keeping away many forms of evil, especially during the dark hours. It is said to repel negative influences, keep witches at bay, fend off robbers, and deter anyone with wicked or envious intent. For this reason single heads or wreaths of garlic have been hung over the top and on the outside of doors, cut cloves have been rubbed on windowsills and doorknobs, and garlic powder has been scattered over floors. In the 16th century, the Flemish botanist Clusius described miners taking garlic to their underground workings to repel the evil spirits who lived there. Cloves of garlic have been worn to protect individuals

Garlic's warming properties led it to be associated with Mars, the god of war and fire. This statue of the god is now in the Museo Capitolino in Rome.

from the evil eye, demons, and monsters—a custom that persists in many parts of the world. The Sanskrit name for garlic means "slayer of monsters." Another form of protection is to carry a clove of garlic and to take a bite of it whenever you sense evil approaching. In Homer's story of Odysseus, the "yellow garlic" the hero was advised to eat by the god Hermes saved him from being turned into a pig like his companions by the witch Circe.

Garlic cloves have been worn or carried by travelers to shield them from the many hazards of the road. Mountaineers carry them to stave off bad weather, and sailors to guard against shipwreck. In the Middle Ages, soldiers wore garlic in the belief that it would deflect the blows of their enemies.

A gift of garlic from a lover might seem a strange token, but garlic is said to induce lust, so be careful who you accept it from! Once wooed, brides in some countries have carried a clove of garlic in the pocket of their wedding dress to bring them good luck.

In Sicily, garlic was put into the beds of women in childbirth, supposedly to avert evil influences from them and the newborn. Once the baby was safely delivered and placed in its cradle, mothers in many countries set garlic and other protective herbs and substances, such as salt and iron, around the cradle, to safeguard the child until baptism.

This mid-19th-century print shows mountaineers climbing Mont Blanc in France. Climbers used to carry garlic in the belief it would keep away bad weather.

Sailors carried many talismans to keep them safe on long sea voyages. They believed that garlic would prevent their ship being wrecked. The moon is shown overlooking sailors in this illustration from a 15th-century manuscript. Just as the ancient Greeks offered garlic to appease the moon goddess Hecate, so sailors carried garlic as a request for protection.

Garlic in Your Dreams

If you dream of receiving garlic it is a sign of coming good fortune; but if you dream of giving it away, you may soon be giving away all your good luck.

Despite its protective qualities, garlic has been viewed by some schools of religion with suspicion as the odor is believed to be associated with the devil and unclean thoughts. This has been the attitude of certain followers of Christianity, Hinduism, Islam, and Zen Buddhism. Many shamans in present-day Nepal are forbidden to eat garlic at all. This mainly applies to the Brahman and Chetri castes, who believe if they eat garlic in the three months before they die, they will not fare well in the afterworld.

Even in ancient Greece, where garlic was offered to Hecate, worshipers were forbidden to eat it before entering the temples of Cybele, mother of the gods, in case their odorous breath offended her, or inhibited any magical work that was to occur.

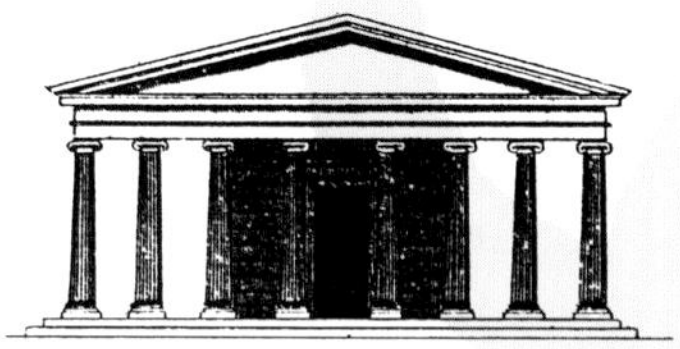

Garlic was not allowed inside temples dedicated to the Greek goddess Cybele.

FOLK MEDICINE

Garlic is one of the most therapeutic plants in existence and, as with many other herbs and methods of healing, medicine, and magic frequently combine in its use. These are just a few of the many garlic folk cures:

- Wear a bulb of garlic around your neck to give you the plant's strength, just as Greek athletes and Roman soldiers did.
- To cure measles, take a piece of linen spun at home and tear it into nine pieces. Use powdered garlic made from nine cloves and spread it on the linen strips. Wrap each piece around the sufferer and leave them for nine days. Bury the linen in the garden and as it rots, the patient will be cured.
- Making the sign of the cross with garlic will charm away certain kinds of tumor according to Sicilian lore.
- Put cloves of garlic in a child's socks to ease whooping cough. This may not entirely be an old wive's tale, since a cut clove of garlic rubbed on the soles of the feet has been found to soothe bronchial troubles.
- Prevent jaundice or hepatitis by wearing a necklace of 13 cloves of garlic around your neck for 13 days. On the last day, walk to a crossroads, take off the necklace, and throw it behind you. Run away without looking back.
- To rid the body of disease, rub a cut clove of garlic on the infected part and throw the clove into running water.

Plant cures were often developed by what is now termed "sympathetic medicine," whereby a plant that resembled a certain organ of the body was thought to provide the most effective means of treating that organ. In a book entitled *Apperatus Planterum*, we read: "The tissue of garlic is ruddy: it expels blood. It has a hollow stalk, and it helps affections of the wind-pipe."

A demon shown tormenting a soul in the 1863 Dictionnaire Infernal. *Rubbing cloves of garlic over doors and around windows was supposed to keep away such demons and evil spirits.*

Islamic Legend

When Satan walked out of the Garden of Eden, garlic sprouted from the ground where his left foot rested and onions appeared in the prints of his right foot.

Roman soldiers, when embarking on a long march or going into battle, wore a bulb of garlic around their necks to give them strength. This Roman pavement mosaic is from the 1st or 2nd century A.D.

FOOD MAGIC

Besides its healing properties, garlic is, primarily, an excellent cooking ingredient, and food and magic have also been long associated. The earliest surviving Chinese text, the *Shih Ching* or *Book of Songs*, which was written in 600 B.C., tells of the spring lamb sacrifices. All through the winter months, the men had hunted animals for furs and meat. After the spring plowing, there was a rite of expiation in which a lamb was sacrificed, seasoned with garlic, and barbecued over a bed of southernwood. The *Shih Ching* says:

High we load the stands,
The stands of wood and earthenware.
As soon as the smell rises,
God on high is very pleased:
"What smell is this, so strong and good?"

There is a belief that rubbing garlic around pots and pans before you start to cook with them will remove negative influences that might contaminate the food. This may have originated from the fact that garlic is a natural disinfectant, and a quick rub with a garlic clove could cleanse the pan of any bacteria.

In France, it was long believed that eating garlic could prevent drunkenness. The newly born Henri IV of France had his lips rubbed with garlic; his grandfather, who carried out this ceremony, was probably combining the old belief that garlic would ward off evil with his wish that the baby should grow into a man with a clear, strong head for rule. Henri grew up to be a great garlic lover and was said to have had "a breath that could fell an ox at 20 paces!"

Garlic and Magnets

It was thought by ancient philosophers and writers, including Pliny, that a magnet of lodestone would lose its powers if it was brought into close contact with garlic.

According to ancient Greek legend, Magnes, a shepherd, discovered magnetite, a magnetically polarized mineral, on Mount Ida when his shepherd's crook was drawn to it while he was tending his flock. People later believed that garlic would remove magnetic powers.

In legend, vampire bats are supposed to turn into blood-sucking fiends during the hours of darkness. Eating garlic gives protection against them. It was believed that the vampires would not be able to drink blood tinged with garlic.

The character of Dracula, the best-known of all vampires, was based upon a 15th-century Balkan nobleman, Vlad Dracul, who lived in the Transylvanian Castle of Bran in Romania.

Garlic and Vampires

Vampires hate garlic. That is a legend known all over the modern world, due largely to books and films. But where did it all begin?

The vampire myth is relatively new. Legends of evil blood-sucking creatures date back to ancient times, but vampires as we know them did not make their appearance until the 16th century, when stories about them began to emerge from the Slavic regions and Balkan states of eastern Europe. The name derives from various eastern European words, including the Magyar *vampir*, which means an animated body supposed to leave the grave at night with evil intent.

Once told, vampire tales were quickly spread by travelers, and a description of vampires was recorded in the 17th century by a Greek writer called Leoni Allaci. In 1746, a French monk, Dom Augustin Calmet, published a learned treatise on the subject which further fueled the rapid spread of the myth.

Vampires were thought to take on human or semihuman forms. This illustration by the 19th-century artist Ernest Griset shows a Baital, an Indian vampire, disappearing through the darkness.

Coming as they did from remote castles and stark winter landscapes, vampires perfectly suited the taste for scary Gothic tales that flourished in the 1790s and continued well into the 19th century. Goethe, Byron, Southey, and Baudelaire all wrote vampire verses; the first European play about vampires was staged in Paris in the 1820s; a singing vampire entertained German opera audiences in 1828; Alexandre Dumas wrote another vampire stage play in the 1850. Gradually, all Europe developed vampire mania.

Melodramatic vampire stories were very popular in the late 19th century. This illustration, entitled "The Feast of Blood" is from Varney the Vampyre*; clearly the victim has not eaten enough garlic!*

It was in 1897 that Bram Stoker wrote *Dracula*, the classic vampire story, which was adapted for the London stage in 1925 and subsequently became the basis of countless books, plays, and films. The name Dracula came from a sadistically cruel 15th-century Balkan nobleman nicknamed *Dracul*, which means "devil" in Romanian, and the story was based on a number of vampire legends.

One strand common to many of the legends is that, besides silver and the cross, vampires hate garlic. During the day, they are entirely at the vampire hunter's mercy, but at night vampires can be overcome with these three essential weapons. To keep vampires out of the house, garlic flowers should be placed on windowsills and cut cloves rubbed around all entrances. A potential victim should wear a string of garlic flowers or bulbs around the neck. To prevent a dead man from becoming a vampire, a wreath of garlic should be placed on his grave.

Whatever the origins of all these myths, the common thread running throughout is that garlic will protect the user from harm, whether in the form of a demon, a vampire, or illness.

Preparing Garlic

It is the way in which you prepare garlic for cooking that affects its ultimate flavor, rather than the amount you use.

Crush two cloves of garlic and add them to a casserole, and you will find that the garlic flavor is strong. If you put in ten whole cloves, the flavor will be milder.

Peeling Garlic

Although some recipes, such as those for roasting whole cloves, require the garlic to be unpeeled, most call for the thin, dry outer layer of skin to be removed. To peel garlic using a small kitchen knife, first cut away the hard root portion from the bottom end of the clove. Some of the skin will come away with this part. The rest can then be eased off with the knife.

If you dislike the smell of garlic on your fingers, you can buy a garlic peeler which will do the job for you.

Bruising Garlic

Some recipes call for cloves of garlic to be bruised. To bruise garlic, first peel it, then hit it once with a heavy implement, such as a rolling pin, so that the skin breaks. Bruise it only; do not squash it flat. Bruised garlic is added whole to dishes, sometimes in quite large quantities. It gives a mild, nutty flavor.

Slicing and Chopping Garlic

Garlic can be sliced crosswise or lengthwise, depending on the type of food and the cooking method you are going to use. Crosswise slices are more often used for stir-fried dishes and casseroles. Lengthwise slices are used for inserting into meats, such as a leg of lamb.

To chop garlic into finer pieces, first slice it on a chopping board. Take a heavy kitchen knife, hold the top of the blade at both ends and bring it

down on the garlic in short, sharp strokes until it is chopped finely enough for your requirements. Alternatively, use a mezzaluna, a curved chopping knife with a handle at each end.

Crushing Garlic

Crushing garlic brings out the strongest flavor and is suitable for salad dressings, stir-fried dishes, marinades, and garlic bread. First, chop the garlic and leave it on the chopping board. Choose a kitchen knife with a thin, flexible blade and, using the tip of the knife, mash the chopped garlic to a purée. Alternatively, chopped garlic can be crushed with a mortar and pestle. A pinch of salt will draw out the juices and make it easier to crush, particularly if the garlic is on the dry side. However, care must be taken when adding salt so as not to spoil the final flavor of the dish. Various types of press can be bought, though it can take longer to use and clean a press than to crush garlic with a knife.

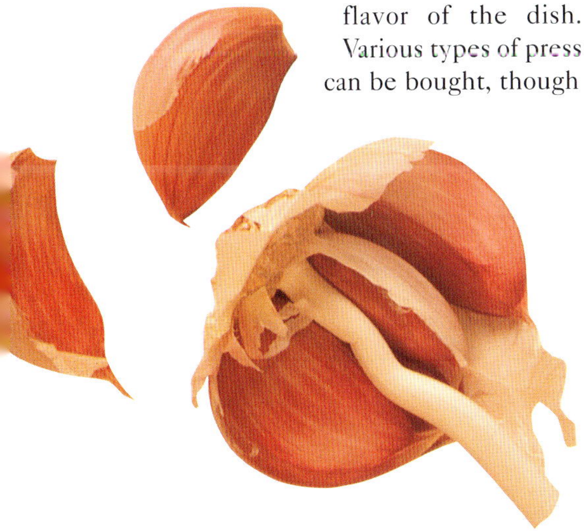

Roasting Garlic

Whole garlic bulbs, roasted very slowly in an oven, acquire a soft consistency and a mild, nutty flavor. You can buy special garlic roasters, usually made of terracotta, which will roast garlic perfectly every time.

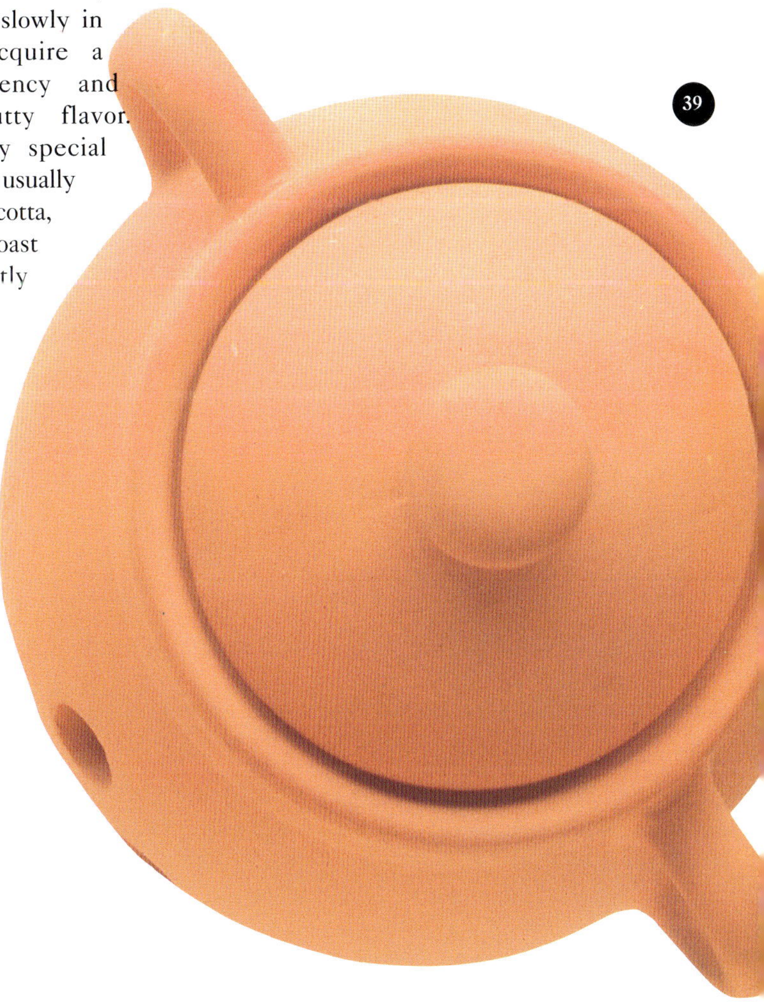

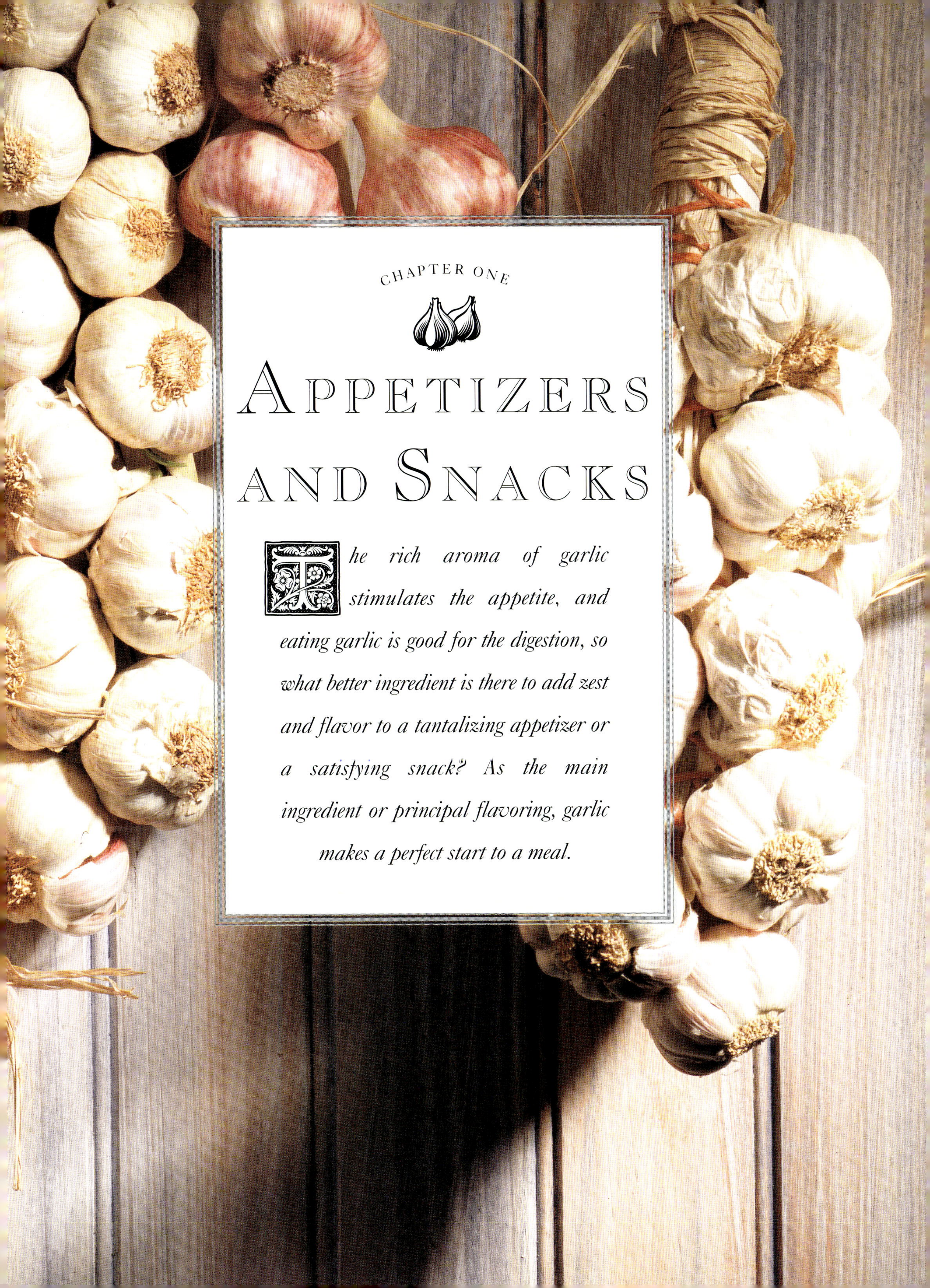

CHAPTER ONE

APPETIZERS AND SNACKS

The rich aroma of garlic stimulates the appetite, and eating garlic is good for the digestion, so what better ingredient is there to add zest and flavor to a tantalizing appetizer or a satisfying snack? As the main ingredient or principal flavoring, garlic makes a perfect start to a meal.

Appetizers and Snacks

Garlic can transform simple dishes into taste extravaganzas. Jumbo Shrimp, *for example, gently sautéed in butter, become a warm and spicy dish with the addition of crushed garlic and chilies, and garlic will lift the flavor of a* Spinach and Cheese Tart. *Warming and nourishing,* French Garlic Soup *is a simple, yet stunning traditional, dish from Provence.* Garlicky Pasta Soup *from Italy is a filling alternative, and the addition of the garlic makes it wonderfully appetizing; in fact, all types of pasta, noodles, and gnocchi benefit from a garlic-flavored sauce. For a special occasion, a* Garlic Soufflé, *made with a whole bulb of roasted garlic, will grace any table. Alternatively, try the informal style of* Potato Skins *with various garlic-flavored fillings.*

The Harvesters, *Pieter Bruegel the Elder, 1565*

Filled Potato Skins

Filled potato skins are great to serve for a casual night in with friends. Each of the three toppings described here is delicious, with plenty of garlic to keep the vampires away!

SERVES 4

3 large potatoes, scrubbed
Vegetable oil for frying
Salt

SPICY CHICKEN FILLING

1tbsp vegetable oil
1 garlic clove, crushed
1 boneless, skinless chicken breast half, thinly sliced widthwise
Freshly ground black pepper
1tbsp soy sauce
2tbsp plain yogurt
1tbsp chopped fresh cilantro

CREAMY MUSHROOM FILLING

2tbsp butter
1 onion, thinly sliced
1 garlic clove, crushed
roughly chopped button mushrooms
3tbsp cream cheese, softened

SHRIMP AND HERB FILLING

3tbsp mayonnaise
2tbsp sour cream
1tsp lemon juice
½ garlic clove, crushed
2tsp chopped fresh dill
2tsp chopped fresh basil

Preheat the oven to 400°F. Prick the skins of the potatoes and bake for 1 to 1¼ hours until tender.

Meanwhile, make the fillings. For the chicken filling, heat the oil in a wok or small skillet. Add the crushed garlic and fry for 30 seconds. Add the sliced chicken and stir-fry for 1 minute. Add plenty of black pepper and the soy sauce and fry until the chicken is golden. Remove from the heat and stir in the yogurt and cilantro. Set aside.

For the mushroom filling, melt half the butter in a small pan. Add the onion slices and fry for several minutes, until crisp and golden. Set aside. Melt the remaining butter in a pan and sauté the crushed garlic for 30 seconds. Add the chopped mushrooms and sauté for 4 minutes longer. Mix with the onion and keep warm. For the shrimp filling, put all the ingredients, except the shrimp, in a small bowl and mix well.

Once the potatoes are cooked, remove them from the oven and allow them to cool slightly. Cut each potato in half lengthwise and scoop out most of the flesh, leaving about ½in of flesh still attached to the skins; reserve the scooped-out flesh for mashed potato or potato cakes another time. Cut each potato in half again, lengthwise.

Pour the vegetable oil into a saucepan, to a depth of about 3 inches, and heat until a cube of bread browns in 30 seconds. Add the potato skins a few at a time and fry for 1½ to 2 minutes, until golden. Drain on paper towels and keep warm while frying the remaining skins. Sprinkle each potato skin lightly with salt. Divide the herb filling between 4 potato skins; top with the shrimp. Spread 4 more skins with cream cheese, then top with the mushrooms and onions. Fill the remaining skins with the spicy chicken mixture. Serve immediately.

Garlic Shops and Information

Specialist garlic shops exist, and there are mail-order firms who specialize in garlic, garlic products, and garlic equipment. From these sources it is possible to buy garlic and garlic-flavored sauces, mustards, marinades, oils, chewing gum, candy, and ice cream (stores only), as well as garlic beauty products and garlic pills and perles. There are also garlic crushers, peelers, roasters, and storage pots and, of course, braids and wreaths of garlic.

Bruschetta *with* Roasted Vegetables

Bruschetta can be served as a simple snack at any time of the day. Or why not prepare some for an evening of al fresco dining, or for a picnic? A multitude of toppings can be used, including artichoke hearts, steamed asparagus spears, and dry cured prosciutto ham.

MAKES 12 BRUSCHETTA

1 small eggplant
Salt and freshly ground black pepper
2 small red bell peppers
2 small yellow bell peppers
7tbsp olive oil
6 garlic cloves
1 zucchini
3 thin slices of prosciutto, cut into 1-inch pieces
1 large French bread
15 ripe pitted olives, finely chopped
1tbsp chopped fresh parsley
6 cherry tomatoes, quartered
6 fresh basil leaves, roughly torn
Small block of Parmesan cheese

Preheat the oven to 400°F. Slice the eggplant in half and then into ½-in slices widthwise. Put the slices in a colander and sprinkle them with salt. Leave to drain over the sink. Cut each pepper in half, de-seed, and cut each half into four pieces. Pour 2 tablespoons of the oil into a roasting tray and heat on top of the stove. Add the peppers and three of the garlic cloves, cut into eighths. Mix together well to coat evenly in the oil. Cover with foil and roast in the oven for 20 minutes. Then remove the foil and roast for a further 15 minutes.

Crush the remaining three garlic cloves and mix them in a small jug with the remaining olive oil.

Rinse the eggplant slices under cold running water and pat them dry on paper towels. Heat 1 tablespoon of the garlic oil in a large skillet. Add the eggplant slices, in batches if necessary. Fry on both sides until golden, adding a little more oil if the pan becomes too dry. Once cooked, remove to a warm plate and keep warm.

Meanwhile, prepare the zucchini. Use a potato peeler to make zucchini ribbons, peeling the zucchini into ribbon-like strips until you reach the seeds. Heat another tablespoon of the garlic oil in a skillet. Add the zucchini ribbons. Stir-fry for a minute and then season with salt and black pepper, remove from the pan, and keep warm. Without cleaning the pan, add the prosciutto and fry it until crisp. Remove from the pan and keep warm.

While the zucchini and prosciutto are frying, preheat the broiler to high. Slice the French bread into 12 pieces, on the diagonal. Sprinkle over the remaining garlic oil and broil on both sides until toasted.

To assemble the bruschetta, take 4 slices of bread and top each with the pieces of red pepper, fried prosciutto, and chopped olives. Sprinkle the chopped parsley over. Take 4 more pieces of bread and top with the yellow pepper, cherry tomatoes, and torn basil leaves. Top the remaining 4 pieces of bread with the slices of eggplant, zucchini ribbons, and shavings of Parmesan, made using a potato peeler. Season all the bruschetta with pepper and then arrange them on a serving platter. Serve immediately.

TAGLIATELLE *with* GARLIC, OLIVE OIL, BASIL, *and* PINE NUTS

Although this pasta dish has a light sauce, it is still bursting with flavors. It contains all the essential ingredients of real Italian cooking: pasta, olive oil, basil, and Parmesan cheese. The garlic is used to impart flavor to the olive oil and is discarded before the dish is served.

SERVES 4 AS AN APPETIZER OR 2 AS A MAIN COURSE

7oz green and white tagliatelle, fresh or dried
8 garlic cloves
6tbsp olive oil
3tbsp pine nuts, toasted
Handful of fresh basil leaves, roughly torn
⅔ cup Parmesan cheese, coarsely grated

Cook the pasta in a large pan of boiling water for approximately 8 minutes if fresh or 12 minutes if dried. Drain it, return it to the pan, and keep it warm.

Meanwhile, bruise the garlic, using the palm of your hand or the back of a spoon. Heat the oil and garlic in a pan very gently for about 5 minutes, stirring occasionally. The garlic should brown but be careful not to burn either the garlic or the oil. Remove the garlic and discard it.

Pour the oil over the tagliatelle. Stir in the toasted pine nuts and transfer to individual warmed serving dishes. Scatter the torn basil leaves and grated Parmesan cheese over. Serve immediately, accompanied by a green salad and some crusty bread.

"To be sure, 'tis not for Ladies' Palates, nor those who court them . . ."

JOHN EVELYN, *ACETARIA: A DISCOURSE OF SALLETS*, 1699

THAI-STYLE FISH CAKES

Garlic is an indispensable ingredient in Thai cooking and is found with the other favorite Thai ingredients—lemongrass, cilantro, and chilies—in these spicy fish cakes. They are ideal as a first course, for handing around at a buffet party or simply as a light snack. If serving at a buffet, provide toothpicks for picking up and dipping the fish cakes in the cucumber relish.

SERVES 4 (MAKES ABOUT 24 MINI FISH CAKES)

3 garlic cloves, chopped
1-in piece of fresh gingerroot, peeled and chopped
2 scallions, sliced
1tbsp sliced lemongrass
1 small fresh red chili, seeded and chopped
12oz skinless cod fillet, cubed
1tbsp Thai fish sauce (optional)
1 egg, beaten
2tbsp chopped fresh cilantro
Salt and freshly ground black pepper
Oil for deep-frying

RELISH (OPTIONAL)
5tbsp rice-wine vinegar or white vinegar
3tbsp sugar
½tsp salt
6 thin cucumber slices, finely chopped
1 scallion, finely sliced
1 fresh green or red chili, seeded and thinly sliced

First make the cucumber relish, if using. Place the vinegar, sugar, and salt in a saucepan and heat gently, until the sugar and salt dissolve. Remove from the heat and allow to cool, then add the chopped vegetables.

To make the fish cakes, place the garlic, ginger, scallions, lemongrass, and chili in a food processor and blend to a purée. Add the fish and blend to a coarse texture. Add the Thai fish sauce (if using), egg, cilantro, and seasoning and purée until smooth.

Heat the oil over a medium-high heat. Take a level teaspoonful of the mixture and then place a second teaspoon, flat-side down, on top of the first, to form a rounded shape. Repeat with the remaining mixture. Carefully drop the rounds into the hot oil, a few at a time. Fry for 1½ to 2 minutes until they float to the surface and are golden brown. Remove with a slotted spoon and drain on paper towels.

Serve the fish cakes at once, dipping them into the cucumber relish if desired.

GARLIC *and* CHILI SHRIMP

If possible, this dish should be made with raw tiger prawns with their shells still on. If these are not available, use cooked jumbo shrimp, and reduce the cooking time by a minute or so, otherwise the shrimp will be tough. Provide your guests with finger bowls and plenty of napkins; this is a messy but delicious dish to eat!

SERVES 4

4tbsp butter
2tbsp olive oil
3 garlic cloves, crushed
1 large, fresh red chili, seeded and finely sliced
16 raw tiger prawns or cooked jumbo shrimp, in their shells
3tbsp finely chopped fresh parsley
Crusty bread, to serve

Heat the butter and oil in a skillet. When the butter has melted, add the garlic and chili. Sauté for 1 minute, without browning the garlic. Add the prawns or shrimp and cook for 4 to 5 minutes; do not cook for longer.

Divide the prawns or shrimp between 4 warmed serving dishes and sprinkle with chopped parsley. Serve with plenty of crusty bread to mop up the garlic-butter sauce.

"Our apothecary's shop is our garden full of pot-herbs, and our doctor is a clove of garlic."

Anonymous, 1615

Garlicky Pasta *and* Bean Soup

This recipe is based on the traditional Italian soup called *pasta e fagioli,* which you will find on many restaurant menus. The soup's flavor will be greatly enhanced if a good-quality chicken stock is used for the broth.

SERVES 4

1tbsp olive oil
1 onion, finely chopped
4 garlic cloves, crushed
14-oz can of canellini beans, drained and rinsed
2 quarts chicken or vegetable stock
1 cup small pasta shapes or spaghetti broken into small pieces
Salt and freshly ground black pepper
Crusty bread, to serve

Heat the oil in a large saucepan over medium heat. Add the chopped onion and sauté it gently for about 3 minutes without allowing it to brown. Add the crushed garlic and continue to sauté for 2 minutes longer. Add the canellini beans, stock, pasta, and seasoning and bring to a boil. Reduce the heat and simmer for 10 to 15 minutes.

Transfer to a warmed soup tureen and serve with plenty of crusty bread.

Dolcelatte *and* Spinach Filo Tart

This is a delicious tart, suitable for eating hot, warm, or cool. Serve it as a light appetizer or add a green salad or vegetables and serve it as a more substantial meal.

SERVES 4

1tbsp olive oil
4 shallots, finely chopped
4 garlic cloves, crushed
7oz fresh spinach, washed and stems removed
6oz dolcelatte cheese, crumbled
2 eggs, lightly beaten
5tbsp heavy cream
Salt and freshly ground black pepper
1½tbsp butter, melted
About 2oz filo pastry sheets

Preheat the oven to 375°F. Heat the oil in a large saucepan and sauté the shallots and garlic very gently until soft.

Meanwhile, place the spinach in a large pan (with no water), cover, and cook for a few minutes until it has wilted. Once cooked, drain the spinach in a strainer, squeeze out as much of the liquid as possible, and roughly chop it.

Stir the cheese into the shallots and cook for one minute longer until the cheese has melted slightly. Remove from the heat and stir in the spinach. Beat together the eggs and cream, then season with salt and pepper and add to the spinach mixture, stirring well.

Lightly grease a 7in diameter, 1in deep, loose-bottomed tart pan with some of the melted butter. Cut the pastry dough into 8 pieces, approximately 8 × 11 inches. (If the filo you are using does not match these dimensions, simply cut it as near as possible and continue as described, using a few extra sheets if necessary.)

Take one sheet of filo and brush it with melted butter. Lay it across half the pan, leaving the edges hanging over the sides. Brush a second piece with butter and use it to cover the other half of the pan. Rotate the pan 90 degrees and repeat with 2 more pieces of filo, brushing each one with butter. Turn the pan twice more, 90 degrees each time, and repeat with the final 4 pieces of filo.

Place the tart on a baking sheet. Spoon the spinach mixture into the pan and scrunch the edges of the filo together. Bake for 20 minutes, until the pastry is golden and the filling is set.

To serve, carefully remove the tart from the pan and serve accompanied by a green salad or vegetables.

Garlic Butter and Bread

Garlic bread is simple to make and standard garlic butter can be combined with other ingredients, such as olives and herbs, to make very exciting, quickly made breads. Here we show how to make a standard garlic butter and give other options. There are also ideas for slightly different garlic breads, such as garlic rolls and garlic pizza-dough. Once the butter is made, store it in an airtight container in the refrigerator and, as long as you use fresh butter, it will keep for 2 to 3 weeks.

Garlic Butter

1

This is the basic recipe, which can be flavored with a wonderful range of ingredients to produce savory butters to go with any kind of meat, fish, vegetable, or pasta.

½ cup butter, at room temperature
3 garlic cloves, crushed

Soften (but do not melt) the butter by beating it in a bowl with a wooden spoon. Stir in the garlic, mixing well. Lay a piece of plastic wrap on the counter and spoon the butter onto it in an oblong shape. Carefully wrap up the butter and roll it to form a fat tube, approximately 6in long. Place in the refrigerator to harden. When required, unwrap the butter and cut slices from it.

Garlic and Herb Butter

2

This is the most popular variation on the standard recipe. Vary the herbs to suit the food you are serving it with; for example, serve tarragon butter with chicken.

½ cup butter, at room temperature
3 garlic cloves, crushed
1tbsp chopped fresh parsley
1tbsp snipped fresh chives

Follow the garlic butter method, mixing the herbs in with the garlic.

Garlic, Olive, *and* Tomato Butter

3

A flavored butter with the characteristic tastes and colors of the Mediterranean.

½ cup butter, at room temperature
3 garlic cloves, crushed
8 pitted ripe olives, finely chopped
3 pieces sun-dried tomatoes in oil, drained and finely chopped

Follow the garlic butter method, mixing all the flavorings in with the garlic.

GARLIC FRENCH BREAD

4

The perfect party and barbecue accompaniment—always make more than you think you will need!

1 long French bread
1 quantity garlic butter

Preheat the oven to 375°F. Cut the loaf into diagonal slices, almost through to the bottom, but so that the loaf still holds its shape. Place a ½-inch slice of garlic butter (approximately) in each cut and then wrap the whole loaf in foil. Bake it for 10 minutes and then remove from the foil and bake it for 5 minutes longer, so the loaf becomes crisp. Serve immediately.

GARLIC PIZZA-DOUGH

5

As an alternative to garlic bread, serve garlic pizza-bases, which are made in minutes and taste really home-made.

5oz (heaped 1 cup) packaged pizza-dough mix
½ quantity garlic butter, cut into small pieces

Make the pizza-dough according to the package directions. Just before baking, scatter half the pieces of garlic butter over the dough, leaving a 1 inch gap around the edge. Once the pizza base is baked, scatter over the remaining pieces of garlic butter. Let it melt slightly for a couple of minutes, then serve immediately.

GARLIC BUNS

6

A wonderful variation on garlic bread, perfect as an accompaniment to home-made soup.

8 small rolls or buns
½ quantity garlic butter

Preheat the oven to 350°F. Slice the tops off the rolls and set aside. Scoop out the filling from the rolls and break it into tiny pieces or process into bread crumbs. Replace the lids on the rolls and put them on to a baking sheet; warm them in the oven for 5 minutes.

Meanwhile, melt the garlic butter in a skillet. Add the bread crumbs and fry for 2 to 3 minutes over high heat, stirring constantly, until the crumbs turns golden. Remove the rolls from the oven. Divide the garlic bread crumbs between the rolls and serve immediately.

FRENCH GARLIC SOUP

This is a traditional Provençal peasant soup, famous for the healing properties the garlic and herbs give it. Traditionally, it was cooked when the larder was empty and there was nothing else to eat. To make the soup stretch farther, chunks of day-old bread were frequently added, along with eggs, poached in the simmering soup.

SERVES 4

12 garlic cloves, peeled
8 fresh sage leaves
5 cups water, with 2tsp salt added
Pinch of saffron strands
4 slices of day-old or toasted bread
2tbsp olive oil
¾ cup grated Gruyère cheese
4 eggs (optional)

Place 11 of the garlic cloves and the sage leaves in a large saucepan with the salted water. Bring to a boil and simmer for 15 minutes. Remove the garlic and sage. Discard the sage and mash the garlic with a mortar and pestle or with a fork. Return the garlic to the cooking liquid, along with the saffron. Keep the soup at a gentle simmer, with the lid on, until ready to serve.

Preheat the broiler to high. Cut the remaining garlic clove in half and rub each slice of bread with it. Then sprinkle each slice with olive oil and top with some grated cheese. Broil until the cheese topping bubbles.

Meanwhile, if serving with poached eggs, carefully add the eggs to the simmering liquid and poach for 3½ to 4 minutes. (An easy way to place the eggs in the water is to crack each egg on to a small plate and then slide the egg off the plate into the water.)

To serve, place a slice of bread in the bottom of individual soup bowls, pour over the hot soup, and, if using, top with a poached egg.

GARLIC SOUFFLÉ

Many people are scared of making soufflés, in case they fail to rise during cooking or rise splendidly only to flop at the last minute. Follow this recipe for a delicious, well-risen soufflé. The secrets are not to open the oven before the cooking time is complete and to have your guests already seated before the soufflé comes out of the oven. This recipe makes either one large soufflé or several small ones.

SERVES 4 TO 6

1 whole garlic bulb
4tbsp butter
4tbsp fresh white bread crumbs
½ cup all-purpose flour
1¼ cups milk
3tbsp finely chopped fresh parsley
Salt and freshly ground black pepper
4 eggs, separated

Preheat the oven to 400°F. Put the whole garlic bulb on a baking sheet and bake it for 40 minutes.

Meanwhile, prepare the soufflé dishes. Either grease one 6¼-cup soufflé dish or 4 to 6 small ramekins with 1 tablespoon of the butter and coat the base and side with bread crumbs. Put the dish(es) on a baking sheet so they are easy to remove from the oven.

Remove the garlic from the oven and allow it to cool slightly; do not turn off the oven. Then carefully squeeze the purée from each clove. Melt the remaining butter in a pan and stir in the flour to make a roux. Cook over low heat for a minute, then gradually stir in the milk, stirring until smooth. Bring to a boil and simmer for a few minutes, stirring constantly, to produce a thick, smooth sauce. Remove from the heat and stir in the garlic purée, parsley, salt and pepper. Beat in the egg yolks, one at a time, and then set the mixture aside.

Whisk the egg whites in a clean, dry bowl until stiff. Using a metal spoon, carefully fold a third of the egg whites into the mixture. Fold in the remaining egg whites and then spoon the mixture into the prepared dish(es). Reduce the oven temperature to 375°F.

Bake the large soufflé for 25 to 30 minutes. After 25 minutes, the soufflé will have a slightly runny center; for a firmer center leave for 30 minutes. Bake the individual soufflés for 10 to 12 minutes. (Do not be tempted to open the oven before this time or the soufflés will collapse.) When cooked, the soufflés should be golden on top and well risen. Seat your guests before removing the soufflés from the oven, then serve immediately.

STUFFED MUSHROOMS

These mushrooms are an ideal appetizer because they can be prepared well in advance. Stuff them several hours beforehand and then bake them just before serving. The garlic butter can also be made ahead of time and spooned around the mushrooms. It will melt during cooking.

SERVES 4

4 large, flat mushrooms, wiped
2tbsp olive oil
4 shallots, finely chopped
3 garlic cloves, crushed
2 fresh red chilies, seeded and finely chopped
1 cup fresh white bread crumbs
Handful of fresh cilantro leaves, roughly chopped
Grated peel and juice of half a lemon

GARLIC BUTTER
4tbsp butter
1tbsp olive oil
2 garlic cloves, crushed
Crusty bread, to serve

Preheat the oven to 400°F. Remove the stems from the mushrooms and roughly chop them. Heat the oil in a saucepan and gently sauté the shallots, garlic, chilies, and chopped mushroom stems for 4 to 5 minutes. Remove from the heat and stir in the bread crumbs, chopped cilantro leaves, and lemon peel and juice.

Meanwhile, melt the butter and stir in the olive oil and crushed garlic. Sauté gently for 3 minutes, without browning the garlic. Divide the filling between the mushrooms. Place the mushrooms in individual baking dishes, just slightly larger than the mushrooms. Pour the garlic butter around the mushrooms, cover each dish with foil, and bake for 10 minutes. Serve hot in the individual serving dishes, with a few slices of bread for mopping up the juices.

Gnocchi *with* Fava-Bean Sauce

Gnocchi are little Italian potato dumplings. Baked in a creamy sauce with fava beans, they make a substantial snack, appetizer, or accompanying vegetable.

SERVES 4

Gnocchi Dough
1lb large potatoes
1 egg, beaten
2tbsp butter
Salt and freshly ground black pepper
1 cup all-purpose flour

Sauce
7oz fava beans
3tbsp olive oil
3 garlic cloves, crushed
¾ cup freshly grated Parmesan cheese
⅔ cup whipping cream, whipped to soft peaks

Preheat the oven to 425°F. To make the gnocchi, prick the skins of the potatoes, place them on a baking sheet and bake for an hour. Reduce the heat to 400°F.

Cut the potatoes in half and immediately scoop out the flesh. Mash with a *mouli-légumes* or a potato masher. Add the beaten egg and butter. Season with salt and plenty of freshly ground black pepper. Mix in enough of the flour to form a firm mixture that does not stick to your fingers.

On a floured countertop, take a quarter of the dough and roll it out into a rope approximately ¾ inches in diameter. Using a knife, cut the dough into pieces at ¾-inch intervals. Dip a fork in some flour and flatten each piece with the back of the fork, working in a curve to give a shell pattern. Transfer the gnocchi to a floured board and repeat with the remaining dough. Keep the prepared gnocchi in a single layer, rather than piling them on top of one another.

Bring a large pan of salted water to a boil and drop half the gnocchi in at a time, ensuring they do not touch. Cook until they float to the surface, 3 to 5 minutes. Remove with a slotted spoon and drain on paper towels. Keep warm while cooking the remaining gnocchi.

To make the sauce, blanch the fava beans in boiling, salted water for 3 minutes. Drain them and, if the skins are tough, remove them by making a small incision in the skin and squeezing gently; the beans should just pop out. Heat the oil in a small pan and gently cook the crushed garlic. Stir in the fava beans, three-quarters of the grated Parmesan, and all the whipping cream.

Grease one large baking dish or 4 individual ones and place the gnocchi in the dish(es). Spoon the fava bean sauce over and sprinkle with the remaining Parmesan cheese. Bake for 10 minutes, until the cheese is bubbling, then serve immediately.

Risotto *with* Garlicky Flounder *and* Spinach

Making risotto the traditional Italian way takes patience, but is well worth the time and trouble. Keep the stock constantly simmering while you make the risotto, taking care not to add more until the rice has absorbed all the liquid in the pan. Serve this delicious dish with some crusty Italian bread and a simple green salad.

SERVES 4

3tbsp olive oil
1 onion, finely chopped
1¼ cups risotto rice (arborio)
2 cups vegetable stock
1¼ cups dry white wine
2tbsp butter
3 garlic cloves, crushed
2 fillets of flounder, cut into strips about 1 × 3in
3½oz spinach leaves, washed and roughly torn
Salt and freshly ground black pepper
Freshly grated Parmesan cheese, to serve (optional)

Heat the stock to simmering. Heat 2 tablespoons of the oil in a large skillet and gently fry the onion for 5 minutes, until soft. Add the risotto rice and stir well; cook for one minute longer. Add a ladleful of the simmering stock and stir well. Once all the stock has been absorbed, add more stock and some of the wine; stir well. Continue adding the stock and wine, a ladleful at a time, until both are used up and the risotto is a creamy mass; do not cover during the cooking process and stir constantly throughout. This should take about 20 minutes. It is important that the rice is allowed to absorb the previous ladleful of liquid before more is added.

Meanwhile, fry the flounder. Heat the remaining tablespoon of oil and the butter in a skillet. Add the crushed garlic and sauté for 1 minute. Then add the pieces of flounder and fry them for about 4 minutes, coating the fish in the garlicky sauce.

Once the risotto is cooked, stir in the torn spinach. Cover the pan with a lid or a large piece of foil and allow the spinach to wilt; this will take about 2 minutes. Scatter the pieces of flounder over the top and serve at once, offering some freshly grated Parmesan cheese, if using.

CHAPTER TWO

VEGETABLES AND SALADS

A vegetable dish can be served as an accompaniment or a meal in itself. Use garlic in a vegetable medley to unite the individual flavors, or with a single vegetable to complement and enhance it. A garlic-based marinade will transform a salad into a feast.

Vegetables and Salads

From warming winter casseroles to fresh summer salads, any type of vegetable dish can be transformed by the addition of a clove, or maybe more of garlic. With a touch of garlic, humble mashed potatoes can be given a special flavor or cold pasta made into an exciting salad, so use it to dress a salad, flavor a marinade or beat into a creamy vegetable purée. Garlic plus different combinations of herbs and spices can give you spicy vegetable dishes from India and the Far East or the colorful, fresh flavors of the Mediterranean. Use garlic whole to flavor roasted vegetables, crushed and mixed with oil either as the base of a mouth-watering dressing, or chopped into vegetable casseroles. Vegetables are one of the most versatile of ingredients and garlic can make them even more so.

Fresco of a fruit and vegetable market at Iffogne Castle, Val d'Aosta, Italian, 15th century

Spicy Vegetable *and* Nut Burgers *with* Chili *and* Tomato Relish

These vegetable burgers are moist and bursting with flavor. Combined with the chili and tomato relish, they will soon become firm family favorites. Serve each burger in a warm bun, accompanied by the relish. The relish will keep for up to three days in the refrigerator.

SERVES 4 (MAKES 4 BURGERS)

1 small green bell pepper, seeded and chopped
2 large garlic cloves, crushed
1 red onion, chopped
½ cup roasted, salted peanuts
¼ cup salted cashew nuts
1 cup fresh white bread crumbs
¾ cup finely chopped shiitake mushrooms
2tsp Thai red curry paste
2tbsp finely chopped fresh lemongrass or 1tsp dried lemongrass
2tbsp finely chopped fresh cilantro or parsley
Freshly ground black pepper
¼ cup all-purpose flour
2tbsp sunflower oil

Relish

1tbsp olive oil
1 garlic clove, finely chopped
1 small fresh red chili, seeded and finely chopped
1 small onion, thinly sliced
6 tomatoes, peeled and cubed
1tbsp red-wine vinegar
1tsp sugar
Salt and freshly ground black pepper

To make the relish, heat the oil in a small saucepan over medium heat. Add the garlic, chili, and onion. Reduce the heat to low and cook gently for about 10 minutes until the onions have softened and slightly caramelized. Add the remaining ingredients, cover, and simmer for 5 minutes longer. Remove the lid, increase the heat, and boil for 5 to 10 minutes longer, stirring frequently, until the relish has reduced and thickened. Keep warm or allow to cool until ready to serve, as preferred.

To make the burgers, put the green bell pepper, garlic, red onion, peanuts, cashew nuts, bread crumbs, and mushrooms in a blender and chop them to a coarse texture. Transfer to a bowl and add the Thai curry paste, lemongrass, cilantro or parsley, and black pepper. Do not add any salt; the salted nuts will provide enough. Combine the mixture well. Divide it into 4 portions, shape each one into a burger, and coat the burgers in the flour.

Heat the oil in a skillet over medium heat and fry the burgers for 5 minutes on each side. Alternatively, broil them under a medium-hot broiler for 5 to 7 minutes on each side. Drain on paper towels and serve immediately in buns with the relish.

Vegetables *in* Thai-Style Coconut-Milk Sauce

Corn-on-the-cob is a delicious vegetable that can be enjoyed far more often than it is. Here it is sliced and added with other vegetables to a spicy sauce. Your guests will have to pick the corn up with their fingers, but it is delicious when coated in the sauce.

SERVES 4

2tbsp sunflower oil
4 garlic cloves, finely chopped
3 shallots, finely chopped
2 small fresh red chilies, seeded and finely chopped
3 cups peeled and dried butternut squash
2 sweet potatoes, each about 12oz, peeled and cut into semicircular slices
14-oz can of coconut milk
2 corn-on-the-cobs
2 zucchini, cut into ¼-in slices

Heat the oil in a large, covered skillet or wok. Add the garlic, shallots, and chilies and stir-fry for 2 minutes, until the shallots are soft. Add the squash and sweet potato and fry for one minute longer, mixing all the ingredients together. Pour in the coconut milk, and bring to a boil, then reduce the heat and simmer, covered, for 10 minutes.

Meanwhile, using a sharp knife, carefully cut each corn cob into 6 pieces and add them to the pan, with the zucchini. Continue to cook for 5 minutes longer. Once all the vegetables are tender, remove them from the heat and serve with boiled rice or noodles.

Garlic is as good as ten mothers.

Ancient Indian proverb

WINTER CASSEROLE *with* CHEESE *and* GARLIC DUMPLINGS

This is a great dish for cold winter evenings. The delicious cheese and garlic dumplings do not use suet, so the whole dish is suitable for vegetarians. Serve with rice or potatoes.

SERVES 4

2tbsp olive oil
2 garlic cloves, crushed
1 onion, cut into eighths and the layers separated
2 carrots, cut into cubes
1 sweet potato, weighing about 12oz, cut into cubes
1tsp hot chili powder
1tbsp all-purpose flour
1tbsp tomato paste
3tbsp Port or dry sherry
1¼ cups vegetable stock
16-oz can of borlotti beans, drained and rinsed
8-oz can of kidney beans, drained and rinsed
1tbsp chopped fresh mixed herbs or 1tsp Italian seasoning
Salt and freshly ground black pepper
3oz small brown mushrooms, quartered
1tbsp finely chopped fresh parsley
Grated cheddar cheese, to serve

DUMPLINGS
¾ cup whole-wheat self-rising flour
¼tsp salt
2tbsp butter, cut into small pieces
2 or 3 garlic cloves, crushed
½ cup grated cheddar cheese
2tbsp chopped fresh parsley
Freshly ground black pepper
4 or 5tbsp milk

To make the dumplings, put the flour and salt in a bowl. Add the pieces of butter and rub them into the flour until the mixture resembles fine bread crumbs. Add the garlic, cheese, parsley, and pepper and mix well. Then add sufficient milk to make a soft, but not sticky, dough. Shape the mixture into 8 dumplings.

To make the casserole, heat the oil in a large casserole dish over medium heat. Add the garlic and onion and sauté gently for 2 minutes. Add the carrots and sweet potato, mix well, and cook for 2 minutes longer, stirring frequently. Add the chili powder, flour, and tomato paste and cook for another minute. Pour in the Port or sherry and cook for a minute. Then pour in the vegetable stock. Add the borlotti and kidney beans, the mixed herbs, and seasoning and stir well. Bring to a boil, then reduce the heat and add the dumplings to the casserole, pushing them well down. Cover with a tightly fitting lid and leave to simmer for 25 minutes. If the lid fails to fit tightly, cover the casserole with a layer of foil before putting the lid on. Add the mushrooms, stir in the parsley, and cook for 5 minutes longer, until all the vegetables are tender. Sprinkle with grated cheddar cheese.

"[The air of Provence is] particularly perfumed by the refined essence of this mystically attractive bulb."

ALEXANDRE DUMAS,
LE GRAND DICTIONNAIRE DE CUISINE, 1873

CELERY ROOT *and* GARLIC PURÉE

Celery root is a vegetable with a delicious flavor all of its own. When mashed with garlic, it makes a delicious accompaniment to meat, poultry, and fish.

SERVES 4

1 garlic bulb
1 celery root, weighing about 1lb 6oz
2tbsp light cream
Salt and freshly ground black pepper

Preheat the oven to 325°F. Put the bulb of garlic on a baking sheet and bake it for approximately 40 minutes.

Meanwhile, chop the celery root into small chunks and put them in a pan of boiling, salted water. Simmer for 10 to 15 minutes, or until it is tender. Drain well.

Allow the garlic to cool slightly, then squeeze the purée from each clove. Transfer the celery root to a blender and purée it until smooth. Add the cream and half the garlic purée and blend for 20 seconds longer. Season well and transfer to a serving dish. Serve hot with roast meats, fish, and other vegetables. Use the remaining garlic purée as a sandwich spread or add to mayonnaise or salad dressings.

The Gilroy Garlic Festival

Take chefs, beauty queens, musicians, jugglers, gourmet food, festival souvenirs, cooking competitions, 4,000 volunteer workers, and 135,000 visitors. Season them with more than 3,000 pounds of fresh garlic, add the Californian sun, and you have the world's largest Garlic Festival—held in Gilroy, California, since 1979.

The idea for the festival originated when Dr. Melone of the local rotary club read of a similar event in Arleux, France. The Gilroy Garlic Festival flourished from the start, and similar events have sprung up in Arizona, Virginia, Washington State, and Canada, but none is bigger or more spectacular than Gilroy. According to fellow founder Don Christopher, now the largest garlic shipper in the world: "It put Gilroy on the map, made garlic more popular."

Tens of thousands of garlic lovers from all over the world flock to Gilroy in the last weekend of July to be treated to a colorful three-day celebration with the scent of their favorite bulb forever wafting in the air.

At the heart of the festival are the food stands. The most spectacular form Gourmet Alley, where local chefs cook on iron pans the size of bicycle wheels over blazing fire pits. Here they prepare huge sirloin steaks and red and green bell peppers for steak-pepper sandwiches, and concoct Garlic Festival Calamari—stir-fried squid with garlic sauce. There is garlic bread, pasta with garlic sauces, and garlic mushrooms, all providing delight for the palate and a feast for the eye. About 3,000 pounds of garlic bulbs are used in the alley alone during the three days of the festival, together with 2,000 pounds of onions, 630 gallons of cooking oil, 1,500 pounds of cheese, and 9,800 pounds of sweet red and green bell peppers.

Other food booths have their own specialties, such as Cajun garlic wings, Italian garlic sausage, or garlic sushi. Trade stands sell garlic by the pound, garlic braids and wreaths, jars of garlic-based sauces and dips, pickled garlic, and garlic olives—even garlic ice cream. You can buy utensils for cooking garlic, as well as the inevitable souvenir T-shirts, refrigerator magnets, and coffee mugs.

Decorative wreaths made from garlic and other spices can be bought at Gilroy, or visitors can learn how to make them at one of the many classes.

Devoted connoisseurs of garlic can enjoy their favorite flavor in this pungent wine.

The blazing pans along Gilroy's famous Gourmet Alley provide a fascinating sight as well as tantalizing aromas.

In Garlic Grove, you can ask the experts any question you like about garlic and its properties. You can learn to top and braid garlic—the two essential skills of harvesting—and take part in topping and braiding competitions. There are cooking demonstrations by well-known chefs and garlic-cooking contests. Live music is everywhere: Cajun, blues, country-and-western, and reggae. Jugglers, puppets, and face-painters entertain the children. There is even a Miss Garlic Festival competition. The winner is chosen not only for her poise and charm but also for her "garlic speech" which she must deliver before a panel of judges.

Garlic braiding classes, contests, and demonstrations are a popular feature throughout the three-day festival.

Pickled garlic, garlic salsa, and garlic mustard—just three of the multitude of garlic products available at Gilroy.

Christopher Ranch, owned by Gilroy Garlic Festival co-founder Don Christopher, is now the largest shipper of garlic in the world.

Even garlic ice cream can be enjoyed at the Gilroy Festival!

The festival officially opens on the preceding weekend with the Garlic Squeeze Barn Dance. In an echo of the Tour de France cycling competition, Gilroy hosts the Tour de Garlique. Other sporting contests which herald the garlic festival include tennis and golf tournaments. A culinary festival based on one small ingredient increases the tourist profile of an entire area.

At the end of the celebrations everyone is happy: visitors, stallholders, organizers, and not least the many local charities and community projects which the festival aims to support. For Gilroy, garlic can well be termed the "universal panacea."

TOMATO *and* ZUCCHINI GRATIN

This is a fresh-tasting, summer dish, reminiscent of the tastes, savors, and flavors of Provence. It is also extremely garlicky, so perhaps should be reserved for friends with a passion for garlic!

SERVES 4

4tbsp olive oil
1 large onion, sliced
2 large zucchini, sliced
3 garlic cloves, crushed
2tbsp finely chopped fresh parsley
6 fresh basil leaves, torn
Salt and freshly ground black pepper
3 large tomatoes, chopped
4tbsp freshly grated Parmesan cheese

Preheat the oven to 400°F. Heat a tablespoon of the oil in a saucepan and gently cook the onion for 5 minutes. Stir in the zucchini and cook for 10 minutes longer, stirring frequently. Meanwhile, combine the remaining olive oil with the garlic, parsley, basil, and seasoning. Transfer the onions and zucchini to a baking dish about 3 inches deep and scatter the chopped tomatoes over. Spoon the oil and herb mixture over and sprinkle with the Parmesan cheese.

Bake for 20 minutes until golden. Serve immediately from the dish.

To Preserve Garlick: Mrs. Gills Receipt

Take three score cloves of large garlick, and put them into a pinte of spring water, and set it on the fire and let them boyle halfe an howre, then take them out, and put them into another pinte of water made redy scalding hott, and let them boyle in it halfe an howre; then take them out of that water, and put them into another pinte of scalding water, and boyle it as before, then take them out haveing your sirrop redy made, to put them into immediately as you take them out of the water, and so boyle them in your sirrop gently, till your sirrop coms to the height [setting point] of other preserves; make your sirrop to preserve them in as follows, take one pounde of the finest pouder suger, and put to it halfe a pinte of spring water, and six spoonfulls of unsett-hisop [hyssop] water, and 3 spoonfulls of the best whitewine vinegar, then set it over the fire, and let it boyle, and scume it, then put in your garlick and preserve it as before directed, then keepe it for your use, this is very good for a cold, or cough; let the party take all this quantity at times, let them take three cloves of garlick every night, and a spoonfull of the sirrop after it, and so let them do till they have taken it all out.

REBECCA PRICE,
THE COMPLEAT COOK,
17TH CENTURY

Garlic Restaurants

Garlic-flavored food has become so popular there are now restaurants all over the world where nothing else is served.

In cities in the United States and Sweden, and in London, you will find Garlic and Shots. *In Los Angeles and San Francisco there are restaurants called* The Stinking Rose, *which boast "We season our garlic with food." Here you can enjoy such dishes as Asparagus and Garlic Soup, Garlic Meat Loaf with Garlic Mashed Potatoes, Garlic and Smoked Mozzarella, and a house salad made with Garlic Vinaigrette and Roasted Walnuts and served with Garlic Bread, plain roasted garlic, and marinated garlic olives. All this can be accompanied by a garlic wine called Château de Garlic, or a garlic beer.*

Spicy Zucchini

This is a quick dish for serving as part of an Indian meal or as a spicy accompaniment to meat and fish. Garlic is widely used in Indian cooking, often mixed with many other spices and herbs to a paste to give an intense, complex flavor.

SERVES 4

2tbsp oil
1tsp black mustard seeds
1tsp cumin seeds
3 garlic cloves, finely chopped
1 fresh red chili, seeded and finely sliced
3 zucchini, weighing about 14oz, sliced
3 tomatoes, skinned and chopped
1tsp ground coriander
1tsp ground turmeric
5tbsp plain yogurt
Handful of fresh cilantro leaves, chopped

Heat the oil in a medium-size skillet. Add the mustard and cumin seeds and cook for 30 seconds until they begin to pop. Stir in the chopped garlic and chili and fry for one minute longer. Add the zucchini slices, tomatoes, coriander, and turmeric. Stir well to ensure that all the pieces of zucchini are coated in the spices. Reduce the heat to a simmer, cover the pan, and cook for 5 minutes until the zucchini are tender.

Stir in the yogurt and let it just warm through; then remove from the heat and stir in the chopped cilantro leaves. Serve immediately.

Eat leeks in Lide [March] and ramsons in May
And all the year after physicians may play.

TRADITIONAL ENGLISH PROVERB

CREAMY MASHED POTATO *with* CRISP BACON BITS

When you are in the mood, there is no better comfort food than this wonderful mashed potato dish. As the whole garlic cloves are boiled first, they lose some of their pungency, so do not worry that it will be too garlicky.

SERVES 4

2lb potatoes, scrubbed, peeled, and quartered
7 garlic cloves, unpeeled
4 slices of bacon
⅔ cup hot light cream or hot milk
Salt and freshly ground black pepper
Knob of butter

Put the potato pieces in a large pan of water, with the garlic cloves, and bring to a boil. Reduce the heat and simmer for 15 minutes, or until the potatoes are tender.

Meanwhile, preheat the broiler to high and broil the bacon until fairly crisp. Then roughly chop the bacon into pieces about ½-inch square.

Drain the potatoes and set aside the garlic cloves. Return the potatoes to the saucepan. Snip the ends of the garlic cloves and squeeze the purée into the potatoes. Mash the potatoes in the pan or remove them, put them through the coarse plate of a *mouli-légumes* and return to the pan. Over low heat, gradually beat in the hot cream or milk and season well. Stir in the bacon and transfer to a warmed serving dish. Top with the knob of butter and serve at once.

SHREDDED CHICKEN SALAD *with* GARLIC-ROASTED PEPPERS *and* CHILIES

All the components of this salad can be prepared in advance so, if you have any leftover chicken, this is the perfect way of using it up. However, the salad is so delicious that it is worth poaching some chicken just for this.

SERVES 4

3tbsp olive oil
4 garlic cloves
1 large red bell pepper, quartered and seeded
1 large yellow or orange bell pepper, quartered and seeded
3 large red chilies, seeded
2½ cups chicken or vegetable stock
Salt and freshly ground black pepper
2 large skinless, boneless chicken breast halves
2oz arugula or other green salad leaves

DRESSING

4tbsp plain yogurt
3tbsp olive oil
1tbsp white-wine vinegar
1 garlic clove, crushed
1tbsp finely chopped fresh mint
Salt and freshly ground black pepper

Preheat the oven to 375°F. Put the olive oil in a shallow roasting pan and heat it gently in the preheated oven or on the stovetop. Bruise the garlic cloves with the back of a spoon and add them to the oil. Add the pieces of pepper and whole chilies to the oil and mix well. Roast for 35 minutes. Once roasted, allow the peppers to cool and discard the garlic.

Meanwhile, pour the stock into a baking dish and season with salt and freshly ground black pepper. Add the chicken breast halves and cover with foil. Poach in the oven for 20 minutes. Remove the breasts from the stock and leave them to cool. Once cooled, shred each breast.

To make the dressing, combine all the ingredients in a screw-topped jar and shake well; set aside.

Place the salad leaves in a large bowl. Once the roasted vegetables have cooled, slice the peppers into strips about ½ inch thick and thinly slice the chilies. Toss together the peppers, chilies, and shredded chicken, then arrange on top of the salad leaves. Shake the dressing again and pour it over the salad and serve at once.

Spinach, Avocado, *and* Mushroom Salad *with* Garlic Croutons

This is a simple but delicious salad, suitable for serving on plenty of different occasions. Try it as an appetizer or a snack or as an accompaniment. It also works well as part of the spread at an *al fresco* party, or serve it on its own for a delicious, light evening meal. Prepare the avocados just before serving, because they will discolor quickly.

SERVES 4

5oz baby spinach leaves
1⅓ cups thickly sliced brown or button mushrooms
2 ripe avocados

Garlic Croutons
2 thick slices of white bread
2tbsp olive oil
2 large garlic cloves, crushed

Dressing
4tbsp olive oil
1tbsp white-wine vinegar
4tbsp heavy cream
2 garlic cloves, crushed
1tsp French mustard

Preheat the oven to 425°F. To make the croutons, cut the bread into cubes about ¼-inch square. Combine the oil with the garlic in a medium-size bowl, add the cubes of bread, and mix well, coating them in the oil and garlic. Transfer to a baking sheet and bake for 5 to 10 minutes, until crisp and golden.

To make the dressing, combine all the ingredients in a screw-topped jar and shake to combine; set aside.

Wash and dry the spinach leaves, removing any stems. Place in a big bowl and add the sliced mushrooms. Peel the avocados, cut each in half and then into cubes. Add the avocado cubes to the spinach and mushrooms and mix well.

Just before serving the salad, shake the dressing once more and pour it over the salad. Top with the garlic croutons and serve immediately.

Shrimp *and* Crab Salad *with* Creamy Garlic *and* Avocado Dressing

This is the perfect appetizer for that special summer dinner with good friends. Although there are several cloves of garlic in the dressing, the flavor is not overpowering and it complements the shrimp and crab.

SERVES 4

2oz salad leaves
8oz crabmeat, fresh or canned
16 cooked, shelled jumbo shrimp, defrosted if frozen

Dressing
5 large garlic cloves, unpeeled
1 large, ripe avocado
4tbsp sour cream
5tbsp olive oil
2tbsp lemon juice
Salt and freshly ground black pepper

To make the dressing, plunge the cloves of garlic into a small saucepan of boiling water and simmer for 20 minutes. Then drain and peel. Place the garlic along with the remaining dressing ingredients into a food processor and blend until smooth.

Divide the salad leaves between 4 serving plates and arrange the crab and shrimp attractively between them. Dribble some of the dressing over and serve immediately. Offer your guests extra dressing in a separate pitcher. Accompany the salad with triangles of buttered whole-wheat bread, if desired.

The Emperor Claudius

The Romans used garlic for many purposes. Soldiers and gladiators ate it to increase their strength and doctors used it successfully as a powerful antibiotic. One of its most infamous uses, however, was as protection against poisoning—something the Roman nobility were constantly on guard against! In 54 A.D. there was a new Roman emperor, Claudius, who married Agrippina, the mother of the infamous Nero. Agrippina persuaded Claudius to adopt her son as his heir and then began plotting to poison her husband so Nero could inherit the throne.

Claudius had a favorite mushroom. His wife arranged for a special dish of these mushrooms to be infused with a lethal poison. One evening, she fed this dish to Claudius, who fell unconscious and had to be carried away from the table. Unfortunately for Agrippina, however, her husband had also eaten quite a number of other dishes, all of which were heavily seasoned with garlic, as well as imbibing vast quantities of wine. Claudius survived the attack, wine and garlic being commonly used as an antidote to poisoning by the Romans.

Agrippina was, however, an extremely resourceful woman. Late that same night she instructed the doctor tending to the sickly Claudius to "tickle the throat of the sufferer with a poisoned feather." This time Claudius was not so fortunate; he died and Nero ascended the throne.

PASTA SALAD *with* MEDITERRANEAN VEGETABLES *and* WALNUT DRESSING

The dressing is garlicky and nutty and makes an ideal accompaniment to the broiled and fresh vegetables. The dressing is also wonderful if you stir it into hot, freshly cooked pasta.

SERVES 4

1 red bell pepper
1 yellow bell pepper
1½ cups pasta quills (penne), fresh or dried
1 small red onion, thinly sliced
8 cherry tomatoes, halved
⅓ cup ripe olives

DRESSING
5tbsp olive oil
2 or 3 garlic cloves, roughly chopped
⅓ cup walnuts
6 fresh basil leaves
2tbsp freshly grated Parmesan cheese
Salt and freshly ground black pepper

Preheat the broiler to high. Broil the red and yellow bell peppers for 10 to 15 minutes, turning them occasionally, until the skins are lightly blackened. Put the peppers in a plastic bag, seal, and leave to cool for 15 minutes (the plastic bag ensures that moisture is retained.)

Meanwhile, cook the pasta in a large pan of boiling water for approximately 8 minutes if fresh and 12 minutes if dried. Drain the pasta and refresh it under plenty of cold running water. Transfer to a bowl.

To make the dressing, put all the ingredients in a food processor and blend for 30 to 60 seconds to chop the nuts finely, rather than purée them.

Remove the peppers from the bag, peel, and seed them, then cut them into slices about ½in wide. Separate the slices of onion and add them to the bowl of pasta with the pieces of pepper, tomato halves, and ripe olives. Combine all the ingredients, then spoon the walnut dressing over and mix well. This salad can be made several hours before serving. Simply cover and refrigerate it. If it is made beforehand, the garlic flavor will intensify.

Garlic Products

Nowadays, garlic is available in many different forms for both cooking and medicinal use, each one with its unique properties.

Garlic Flakes

Garlic flakes are produced by slicing or chopping fresh garlic cloves and putting them through a drying process, turning them into small, creamy colored flakes or pieces. Garlic flakes can be sprinkled into all kinds of cooked dishes that require garlic and should be added before or during cooking so it softens. One scant teaspoon of garlic flakes is the approximate equivalent of one fresh clove. It has a nutty, sometimes caramel-like taste, which, although not powerful, can be used to advantage in garlic-based dishes with a distinctive flavor, such as the Provençal soup *aigo-boulido*. Garlic flakes can also be used medicinally.

Garlic Powder

Garlic powder is produced by grinding dried garlic to a coarse, creamy colored powder. When using garlic powder in the kitchen, sprinkle it into dishes before or during cooking, to give it time to soften before the dish is served. Likewise, allow salad dressings to stand for at least one hour after garlic powder is added, so softening can occur. Half a teaspoon of garlic powder is the equivalent of one medium-sized garlic clove. Its flavor is similar to that of dried garlic. Garlic powder can be used medicinally and is the main ingredient of some garlic tablets.

Garlic Purée

Garlic purée is a thick, white paste made from garlic powder that has been mixed with oil, salt, and a preservative. It can be added to cooked dishes and salad dressings and used to make such things as garlic bread. It has a salty, slightly nutty flavor. Bear in mind the saltiness when flavoring your dishes. About ½tsp of purée is the equivalent of one medium-sized garlic clove. Garlic purée is most suitable for the kitchen, as some of its medicinal properties are destroyed during processing.

Garlic Salt

Using garlic salt, a mixture of finely ground dried garlic and salt, is a quick and easy way to add two important flavors to your food. Care is needed when using garlic salt in cooked dishes such as casseroles and stews, because an over-salty taste is unpleasant. It is excellent for adding to water in which vegetables are being boiled, and for sprinkling over roasted nuts. A pinch can be added to a plain salad dressing and it can also be used in place of ordinary salt for breads and other savory baked goods. Garlic salt is rarely used medicinally.

Garlic Capsules

Garlic capsules, or garlic perles, were reputedly invented by J. A. Höfels, a German doctor who moved to England in 1920. He believed in garlic as a cure for many diseases, and he decided the only way to persuade people to eat it would be to disguise its odor. He, therefore, set about developing a process of extracting the oil from garlic cloves and encapsulating it in a thick, firm, jelly-like edible substance.

To extract the oil from garlic, raw cloves first have to be boiled. This preserves much of the valuable sulfur content of garlic, making garlic perles an effective natural treatment for coughs, viruses, and yeast disorders, such as candida. However, boiling destroys a large part of the garlic's allicin, which is the active ingredient involved in benefits to blood circulation and cholesterol levels.

Garlic Tablets

Garlic tablets are an ideal way of taking garlic medicinally. They are produced by first drying garlic and grinding it to a powder, a process which preserves the allicin. The powder is then formed into small balls and given a hard, edible coating. When the tablets are swallowed, the coating dissolves in the stomach and the beneficial elements of the garlic are absorbed into the bloodstream without producing any odor to exhale through the lungs.

When buying garlic tablets, always aim for the best quality. This is usually determined by price. Garlic from all over the world is used to make tablets and some contain more active ingredients than others. Chinese garlic is said to be the most effective. You can test the quality of garlic tablets by cutting them open and smelling or tasting them. The stronger the aroma and flavor, the more effective the tablets. The best brands are those that undergo quality-control tests to determine the allicin content of the tablets. If this has been done, it will be stated on the package.

CHAPTER THREE

MEAT AND POULTRY

Garlic is used all over the world to flavor every kind of meat and poultry in a great diversity of dishes. From plain roasts and simple salads to spicy curries and rich stews, all meat dishes will benefit from the appetizing savor of garlic.

Meat and Poultry

Meat and garlic are perfect partners. Garlic can give a meat dish a wonderful aroma and taste, whatever the cooking method. A classic roast is both simple and special, and a peeled clove or two of garlic added to the roasting pan at the start of cooking will gently impart flavor throughout the meat. Roast cloves whole for Chicken with 40 Cloves of Garlic *and squeeze out the garlic flesh at the end of cooking to make a natural accompaniment. Insert whole cloves or slices of garlic into a leg of lamb, or garlic slivers into tender duck breasts. Add relish to plainly cooked cold meats by serving them in or alongside a salad tossed in a garlic-flavored dressing.*

Ensure your meat is tender with a delicious tang by steeping it in a garlic-based marinade. Mix the garlic with ginger, papaya, chili, and tomato paste for lamb, and with soy sauce, sesame oil, and ginger to make Teriyaki Chicken *in Japanese style. Curries would not be authentic without garlic, and other slow-cooked stews, such as goulash, or braised meats, such as* Mediterranean-style Pork Chops, *always taste delicious when cooked with garlic. Garlic stuffings can be used for all kinds of meats: mixed with rice and mushrooms, garlic makes a tasty filling for pork tenderloin; combined with ground lamb and rice, it can be rolled up in grape leaves.*

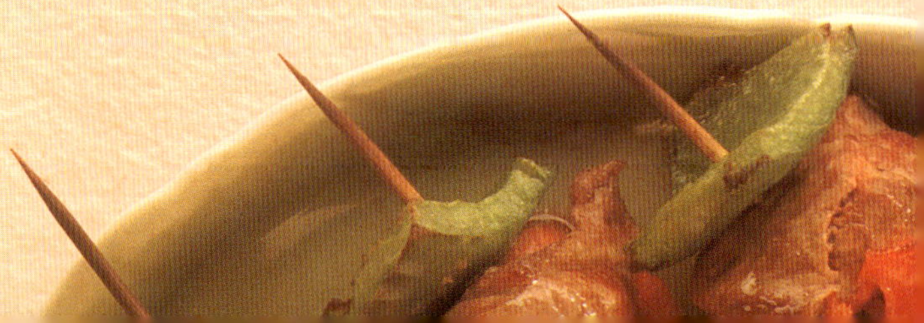

The Fried-Food Seller, *Pietro Longhi, 18th century*

GOULASH *with* GARLIC NOODLES

Shpaetzlen are traditional Jewish noodles eaten with goulash. They are similar to the bow-tie shaped pasta (*farfalle*) you can buy in many supermarkets and delicatessens and it is these which have been used in this recipe. Traditionally in the Jewish faith, meat and dairy products are not consumed at the same meal. However, many people nowadays offer sour cream with goulash.

SERVES 4

2lb lean stewing or braising beef, cut into 1½-in cubes
2tbsp all-purpose flour, seasoned with salt and freshly ground black pepper
3tbsp vegetable oil
1 large onion, sliced
2 garlic cloves, finely chopped
1tsp paprika
1¼ cups tomato juice
2 potatoes, cut into cubes
Salt and freshly ground black pepper
3 cups bow-tie pasta (farfalle), fresh or dried
3tbsp butter
2 garlic cloves, crushed
⅔ cup sour cream, to serve

Toss the pieces of meat in the seasoned flour to coat them lightly. Heat 1 tablespoon of the vegetable oil over high heat in a large casserole. Add the cubes of meat, in two batches, if necessary. Brown the meat and transfer it to a bowl with a slotted spoon. Reduce the heat, add the onion, and cook gently for 10 minutes, stirring frequently. Stir in the garlic and continue to cook for 2 minutes. Return the meat to the pan and sprinkle the paprika over. Cook over low heat for a couple of minutes. Pour in the tomato juice, bring to a boil, cover, and leave to simmer gently for an hour. Stir in the cubed potatoes and continue to simmer for 30 minutes longer, until the potatoes are cooked and the goulash has thickened. Check the seasoning.

At the same time as the potatoes are added to the goulash, bring a large pan of water to a boil and cook the pasta for approximately 8 minutes if fresh or 12 minutes if dried. Drain it, rinse it under boiling water, and transfer it to a warmed serving dish. Melt the butter in a small pan and stir in the crushed garlic. Cook for 1 minute, stirring frequently, without browning the garlic. Pour the garlic butter over the pasta and toss well. When the goulash is cooked, serve the noodles topped with the goulash and hand around a bowl of sour cream separately.

Teriyaki Chicken

This is a Japanese-style recipe and the marinade works equally well with beef and pork. Although the chicken can be left for just 30 minutes to marinate, leaving it for several hours, or even overnight, is preferable. While the chicken is cooking, warm up the marinade and serve it as a rich sauce, with boiled rice.

SERVES 4

4 garlic cloves, crushed
1-in piece of fresh gingerroot, peeled and grated
2tsp sesame oil
½ cup sake or dry sherry
¾ cup soy sauce, preferably Japanese shoyu sauce
2tbsp sugar
½ cup chicken stock
1tsp cornstarch
4 chicken breast halves, cut into 1-in cubes
6 scallions, cut into 1-in pieces
4 shredded scallions, to serve

First, soak 6 to 8 bamboo skewers in cold water for an hour; this prevents them from burning while the chicken is cooking. Alternatively, use metal skewers. To make the marinade, put the garlic, ginger, and sesame oil in a saucepan and heat gently. Cook for a minute and then stir in the sake or dry sherry, soy sauce, sugar, and stock. Bring to a boil and simmer for 10 minutes.

Blend the cornstarch with 1 tablespoon of water and add it to the sauce. Stirring constantly, return the sauce to a boil and then reduce the heat and leave to simmer for 5 minutes, until the sauce thickens slightly. Remove from the heat and allow to cool.

Put the pieces of chicken and scallions in a bowl and pour the marinade over. Mix well, cover, and leave to marinate for at least 30 minutes.

Preheat the broiler to high and then remove the chicken and scallions from the marinade and thread them alternately onto the skewers. Oil the wire rack of the broiler pan and put the kabobs on it. Brush the chicken with the marinade and broil each side for 5 to 6 minutes, brushing with more marinade during cooking.

While the kabobs are broiling, transfer the remaining marinade to a small saucepan and bring to a boil. Reduce the heat and simmer until the kabobs are cooked. Serve the teriyaki chicken on a bed of rice and scatter additional shreds of scallions over. Serve the sauce separately.

Mediterranean-Style Pork Chops

This fresh-tasting dish is quick to prepare and makes a tasty main course for a dinner party. The sauce can be prepared in advance. Serve the chops with rice or potatoes and a green vegetable. Creamy Mashed Potato with Crisp Bacon Bits (see page 71) is a good accompaniment.

SERVES 4

3tbsp olive oil
4 boneless pork loin chops
1 onion, sliced
1 red bell pepper, seeded and cut into thin strips
12 garlic cloves, peeled and bruised with the back of a spoon
3 cups chopped ripe tomatoes, or 14-oz can of chopped tomatoes
¾ cup ripe olives
2 fresh thyme sprigs
Salt and freshly ground black pepper
6 fresh basil leaves

Preheat the oven to 350°F. Heat a skillet thoroughly and add 2 tablespoons of the oil. When this is smoking hot, add the pork chops. Fry them on both sides for 2 minutes, until browned and sealed. Transfer to a baking dish.

Reduce the heat to medium. Add the remaining tablespoon of oil and let it heat up. Add the onion and fry it gently for 5 minutes. Add the slices of red bell pepper and whole garlic cloves. Cook for 5 minutes longer, until the onions and peppers are softened. Stir in the tomatoes, olives, thyme, and seasoning. Mix well. Pour the sauce over the pork chops, cover with foil, and bake for about 20 minutes. Just before serving, roughly tear the basil leaves and scatter them over the dish.

When serving the dish, offer each guest a few cloves of garlic from the sauce.

"Peace and happiness begin when garlic is used in cooking."

Marcel Boulestin, early 20th century

CHICKEN *with* 40 CLOVES *of* GARLIC

Although 40 cloves of garlic may sound like a huge quantity, they are roasted in their skins and impart the most delicious flavor to this classic French dish from Dauphine.

SERVES 4

Large bunch of parsley, thyme, and rosemary
2 bay leaves
1 whole chicken, weighing approximately 4lb
Salt and freshly ground black pepper
7tbsp olive oil
40 garlic cloves, unpeeled
¾ cup all-purpose flour
5tbsp water

GRAVY (OPTIONAL)
1¼ cups chicken or vegetable stock
2tbsp cornstarch
5tbsp light cream

Preheat the oven to 350°F. Form the herbs into 2 bouquet garnis, one slightly smaller than the other. Wash and pat dry the chicken and season inside and out with salt and pepper. Place the smaller bouquet garni in the cavity of the chicken. Pour the oil into a flameproof casserole which is large enough to hold with chicken with the lid on. Add the second bouquet garni and the garlic cloves and gently heat the oil on the stovetop. Add the chicken and turn it to coat it in oil, ensuring the herbs remain beneath the chicken. Mix the flour and water to form a thick paste. Roll the paste into a long rope shape and place this around the edge of the casserole to act as a seal for the lid. Roast for 1½ hours. To serve, either break and clean off the seal before taking the dish to the table, or break the seal in front of your guests, filling the room with a delicious aroma.

If you decide to make the gravy, remove the chicken to a warmed serving dish along with about two thirds of the garlic cloves, then remove and discard the bouquet garni from the casserole. Place the casserole on the stovetop and heat over medium-high heat. Squeeze the purée from the remaining garlic cloves and mix into the cooking juices. Stir in the stock. Mix the cornstarch with 1 to 2 tablespoons of water to form a smooth paste. Add to the casserole, stirring to prevent any lumps. Once the gravy has thickened, add the cream. Heat through and serve.

Thai-Style Sliced Beef

Although this recipe does not include a great deal of garlic, it only takes a solitary clove to lift the dish and, in combination with the other ingredients, to coat the beef with a deliciously tangy dressing. Timings given are for rare beef; if you prefer your meat slightly better done, fry it on both sides for an additional minute or two.

SERVES 4

1 large red bell pepper
2oz arugula leaves
beef tenderloin
1tbsp olive oil

Dressing

5tbsp extra-virgin olive oil
1½tbsp balsamic vinegar
1tbsp lime juice
1tsp mustard powder
1 garlic clove, crushed
1tbsp chopped fresh cilantro
Salt and freshly ground black pepper

Preheat the broiler to high. Put the pepper under it and broil for 15 minutes, turning occasionally. Once the skin is charred, put the pepper in a plastic bag and allow to cool.

Meanwhile, to make the dressing, put all the ingredients in a screw-topped jar and shake well. Once the pepper has cooled, peel away the skin and seed the flesh. Cut the flesh into thin strips and mix them with the arugula leaves.

Put the beef between 2 pieces of waxed paper and use a rolling pin to flatten it to about ⅝in to ¾in thick. Next, heat a skillet. Add the oil and allow it to heat up. Add the beef and fry it on each side for 2½ to 3 minutes. Remove the steak from the pan and thinly slice it diagonally.

To serve, pile the arugula leaves and pepper strips into a serving dish, sprinkle half the dressing over and toss well. Arrange the slices of beef on top of the salad and pour the remaining dressing over. Serve immediately.

ROAST LEG *of* LAMB *with* GARLIC *and* ROSEMARY

The copious amounts of garlic do not overwhelm the flavor of the lamb, but simply infuse it with a light garlic flavor. Add the roasted vegetables, red wine gravy, and mint sauce and the result is a traditional roast that few can resist.

SERVES 4

3lb leg of lamb
10 to 15 garlic cloves, thickly sliced
20 small sprigs of rosemary
1½lb potatoes, peeled and cut into chunks
2 red onions, cut into eighths
2tbsp olive oil
Salt and freshly ground black pepper

MINT SAUCE
2tbsp chopped fresh mint
1tbsp sugar
2tbsp boiling water
3tbsp white-wine vinegar

GRAVY
Pan juices
1tbsp all-purpose flour
3tbsp red wine
1¼ cups vegetable stock
Salt and freshly ground black pepper

Preheat the oven to 350°F. Make small slits all over the skin of the leg of lamb with the point of a sharp knife and put a garlic slice and a sprig of rosemary into each slit. Transfer the lamb to a roasting pan and scatter any remaining garlic slices around the lamb. Arrange the potatoes and onions around the lamb, drizzle with the oil, and season with salt and freshly ground black pepper. Toss the vegetables in the oil, and seasoning until they are evenly coated. Roast for approximately 1 hour 40 minutes (25 minutes per pound, plus 25 minutes extra), or until the meat is cooked to desired doneness; if you prefer pinker meat, omit the final 25 minutes. Transfer the meat (reserving the pan juices) and vegetables to a warmed serving platter and cover with foil to keep warm.

While the lamb is roasting, make the mint sauce. Combine all the ingredients in a small bowl and leave for at least an hour before serving for the flavors to combine.

To make the gravy, skim off and discard all but 1 tablespoon of the fat from the pan juices. Place the roasting pan with the pan juices on the stovetop over medium heat and stir in the flour, scraping up any bits left in the pan. Add the red wine and stock and bring to a boil, stirring to prevent any lumps. Simmer for a couple of minutes and then season with salt and freshly ground black pepper. Transfer to a warm sauce boat or pitcher.

Serve the lamb with the roasted vegetables, gravy, and mint sauce. Add some other vegetables such as peas and broccoli, or try the celery root purée on page 65.

Stuffed Grape Leaves

Stuffed grape leaves are a specialty throughout the Middle East, Greece, and Turkey. As fresh ones are rarely available, buy them preserved in brine. Although poultry is not usually associated with grape leaves, you can substitute ground chicken or turkey for the more usual ground lamb, if you like. Serve as an hors d'oeuvre or as part of a buffet.

SERVES 4 (MAKES 16 STUFFED GRAPE LEAVES)

28 grape leaves
3tbsp olive oil
1 large onion, finely chopped
4 or 5 garlic cloves, crushed
3tbsp short-grain rice
8oz ground lamb, chicken, or turkey
2tbsp chopped fresh mint
2 tbsp chopped fresh parsley
2tbsp currants or raisins
Salt and freshly ground black pepper
⅔ cup lamb, chicken or vegetable stock
1 lemon, cut into eighths, to serve

To prepare the grape leaves, rinse them under cold running water and then drop them into boiling water, a few at a time. Blanch for 3 minutes, then transfer to a bowl of cold water. Drain, pat dry on paper towels and set aside.

Heat 1 tablespoon of the oil in a saucepan over medium heat and gently fry the onion for 5 to 6 minutes, until soft. Add the crushed garlic and fry for 2 minutes longer.

Put the rice, meat, herbs, and currants or raisins in a large bowl and mix well. Stir in the onions and garlic and season well. Put 16 of the leaves shiny side down (veins facing up) on a work surface. Divide the filling between the leaves, placing it in the middle of each leaf. Fold the stem end and sides over the filling and roll up toward the tip of the leaf, to form a roll. Line a small flameproof dish with 6 of the reserved leaves and arrange the stuffed grape leaves in the dish in 2 or 3 layers, sprinkling the layers with the remaining oil. Pour the stock over and cover with the remaining grape leaves. Press down the stuffed grape leaves with a small plate. Cover the casserole, leaving the plate in place, and simmer gently on the stovetop for an hour.

To serve, remove the stuffed grape leaves from the cooking liquid and arrange them on the lining leaves on a platter. Serve hot or cold, accompanied by lemon wedges.

Beef Curry

The garlic and ginger used in this curry give an authentic, fresh flavor, which is so much better than the taste of commercial curry powder. Serve with rice, poppadoms, chutneys, and plain yogurt for an exotic, Indian-style feast.

SERVES 4

1tsp ground coriander
1tsp ground cumin
1tsp ground cinnamon
3tbsp sunflower oil
1½lb lean beef (stewing, braising, or casserole), cut into 1-in cubes
1 large onion, finely chopped
6 or 7 garlic cloves, crushed
2-in piece of fresh gingerroot, peeled and grated
2 fresh red chilies, seeded and sliced
4 cloves
4 cardamom pods
2tsp ground turmeric
1tbsp tomato paste
2 ripe tomatoes, roughly chopped
1 bay leaf
Salt and freshly ground black pepper
4tbsp plain yogurt
2tbsp chopped fresh cilantro

Heat a heavy-based flameproof casserole over medium heat and dry-fry the coriander, cumin, and cinnamon for 30 seconds, stirring constantly to prevent them burning. Transfer to a small plate or bowl. In the same pan, heat half the oil over high heat and brown the meat on all sides. Remove with a slotted spoon and set aside.

Reduce the heat to low, add the remaining oil to the casserole and fry the onion for 10 minutes until soft and golden. Add the garlic, ginger, and chilies and continue to fry for 2 minutes longer. Stir in the dry-fried spices, cloves, cardamom pods, and turmeric and cook for 1 minute longer. Add the browned meat to the pan, stirring well to ensure all the meat is coated in the spices. Cook for 2 minutes. Stir in the tomato paste, tomatoes, ¾ cup of warm water, and the bay leaf. Season well. Bring to a boil, reduce the heat, and leave to simmer, covered, for 60 minutes, or until the beef is tender. If the curry becomes too dry during cooking, add a little more water. Once the curry is cooked, stir in the yogurt and sprinkle the cilantro leaves over it.

Lamb Kabobs

Lamb and garlic are natural partners. Raw green papaya is used in the marinade, but, if there isn't any available, use papaya juice or meat tenderizer instead. Serve the kabobs with rice and salad.

SERVES 4

1½lb lamb tenderloin, cut into 1-in cubes
1 red onion, cut into eighths and segmented
1 red bell pepper, seeded and cut into 1-in squares

Marinade
5 garlic cloves, crushed
1-in piece of fresh gingerroot, peeled and grated
2tbsp finely chopped, raw green papaya or 2tbsp papaya juice or 1tsp meat tenderizer
1tsp hot chili powder
1tbsp tomato paste
1tbsp vegetable oil
Salt and freshly ground black pepper

If using wooden skewers, soak them in water for an hour before cooking so they do not burn. Alternatively, use metal skewers. Combine the marinade ingredients in a bowl to make a paste and add the cubes of lamb. Toss well in the marinade, cover and leave to marinate for at least 6 hours or, preferably, overnight. Thread the cubes of meat onto the skewers, alternating with pieces of onion and pepper. Preheat the broiler to high and oil the broiler rack to prevent sticking. Broil the kabobs for 10 to 12 minutes, turning them occasionally so the meat cooks evenly. Brush with the marinade during cooking.

Garlic and Animals

Garlic has long been regarded as an excellent tonic and treatment for animals. Wild animals seek out all species of garlic, and gorillas actually plant patches of wild garlic near their colony homes.

All over the world, garlic has been fed to farm animals. It is chopped and mixed with bran and molasses for cattle and horses, and for dogs, there are garlic-flavored biscuits. Garlic is considered to act as a general tonic, to cleanse the animals' blood, and to build up a natural resistance to disease. It is also said to improve the performance of bulls and stallions. Cole's *Art of Simpling*—a work on the uses of "simples," or plant remedies, written in the 16th century—says game cocks which have been fed on garlic are "most stout to fight, and so are horses."

Garlic is also a valuable basic veterinary remedy for conditions in which the blood must be cleansed or mucus expelled. It is also used to get rid of worms, to cure mastitis, and to dispel blood clots in the legs of horses. A natural antiseptic, it can be applied externally for disinfecting sores and wounds.

The drawback of treating dairy animals with garlic is that it taints the milk. The way to get around this is to feed with garlic at milking time, so the aroma will have left the bloodstream by the time of the next milking. Cows are very fond of wild garlic, so farmers have to make sure that it is dug up from pastures.

Garlic has also been used to protect animals from evil influences. In Sweden, for example, cloves of garlic were once fastened around the necks of cows and horses to deter trolls who were believed to come by night to steal the milk or ride a horse to exhaustion.

Sport, too, has associated garlic with animals. Jockeys were in the habit of rubbing the horse's bit with garlic or tying a clove of garlic to the bridle to guarantee success in a race. Whether they thought it would help their mount or fend off rivals is uncertain, but Mrs. Grieve, writing in her *Modern Herbal* in 1931, said "Hungarian jockeys will sometimes fasten a clove of garlic

This gleeful little hobgoblin is taken from a 1901 edition of the classic children's story The Snow Queen. *In Sweden, garlic was used to protect farm animals from mischievous trolls and goblins.*

A Dog's Recovery

Mr. W. H. Butlin of Tiptree, Essex, England, records the following experience: "A fox-terrier, aged 14 years, appeared to be rapidly developing a pitiable condition, with a swollen neck and an ugly intractable sore at the root of the tail, and dull, coarse coat shedding abundantly. I administered 'Yadil Antiseptic' [a patent medicine which contained garlic] in his drinking water and in less than a month the dog became perfectly sound and well, mirabile dictu, *his coat became firm, soft, and glossy."*

From the *Morning Post*,
December 12, 1922

Even your pets can enjoy the taste of garlic with these garlic-flavored dog biscuits!

to the bits of their horses in the belief that any other racers running close to those thus baited, will fall back the instant they smell the offensive odor."

Bullfighters carried a clove of garlic, often on a cord around their neck. Some believed it would protect them from the horns of the bull and others that it would prevent the bull from charging at them.

Repelling Unwanted Animals

For centuries, garlic has been used to deter unwanted creatures. The belief that wearing or carrying garlic will ward off scorpions and serpents is an old one. The Egyptian Ebbers papyrus says: "To prevent a snake emerging from its hole, a clove of garlic should be placed at the opening."

Cole's *Art of Simpling* advises that if a garden is infested with moles, garlic or leeks will make them "leap out of the ground presently." Modern gardeners have found that dried garlic powder sprinkled around seedlings will protect them from insects, birds, and moles, and a solution of garlic powder or a strong infusion of crushed garlic is a powerful insect repellent. Researchers at the University of Washington in Seattle have saved thousands of trees from destruction by planting garlic pellets around them to fend off rabbits and deer.

Scorpions should always be treated with caution. In ancient Egypt, garlic was considered an effective repellant if you were unlucky enough to come across one.

The Bullfight *by Eugenio Lucas. Bullfighters believed garlic would stop a bull from charging or, if it did not, would at least protect them from the bull's sharp horns.*

Roasted Duck Breasts *with* Garlic *and* Black Grape Sauce

Duck and fruit are natural partners. Here, duck breasts are roasted with garlic and served with a bold garlic and black grape sauce. A less fatty duck, such as Barbary, is good but other kinds may also be used. Served with new potatoes and green vegetables, this is an ideal dinner-party dish.

SERVES 4

4 small to medium, skinless, boneless duck breast halves
2 large garlic cloves, sliced
1tbsp oil

SAUCE

2tbsp butter
2tsp sugar
2 shallots, finely chopped
2 garlic cloves, crushed
1tsp grated nutmeg
1¼ cups red wine, such as burgundy
6oz black grapes, halved, seeded, and skinned if the skins are tough
Salt and freshly ground black pepper

Preheat the oven to 400°F. Cut several incisions about ½in deep across each breast and insert the slices of garlic. Heat a skillet. Add the oil and fry the duck breasts for 4 minutes, garlic-side up. Transfer to a roasting pan and roast for 15 minutes for rare meat and 20 minutes for medium meat. Once the breasts are cooked, leave them to rest in a warm place, until the sauce is ready.

To make the sauce, melt the butter in a small pan over high heat. Add the sugar and stir until the sugar has melted. Reduce the heat to low, add the shallots, garlic, and nutmeg and cook for 3 to 4 minutes longer. Stir in the wine, bring to a boil, reduce the heat, and leave to simmer for 10 to 15 minutes, until the sauce has reduced by a quarter. Stir in the grapes and season. Cook for 2 minutes longer. Serve each duck breast surrounded by some of the sauce.

PORK TENDERLOIN *stuffed with* GARLIC *and* MUSHROOM RISOTTO

As the risotto in this dish is used as a stuffing, a quick method of making it has been devised so you can use the time saved to prepare the rest of the meal. This is a very special dinner-party dish; enjoy it with roast potatoes and seasonal vegetables.

SERVES 4

1tbsp olive oil
1 small onion, finely chopped
2½ garlic cloves, crushed
⅓ cup risotto rice (arborio)
1 cup chicken stock
½ cup white wine
Salt and freshly ground black pepper
¾ cup finely chopped mushrooms
4 pork tenderloins
2tbsp butter
1tbsp vegetable oil

GRAVY
½ garlic clove
1tbsp all-purpose flour
3tbsp dry sherry
1¼ cups vegetable stock or vegetable cooking liquid
Salt and freshly ground black pepper

Preheat the oven to 350°F. To make the risotto, heat the olive oil in a pan and gently fry the onion for 5 minutes until soft. Add the crushed garlic and cook for 2 minutes; then stir in the rice. Continue cooking for a minute, stirring so all the rice is coated in the oil and onion mixture. Reduce the heat to medium-low and pour in the stock and wine and season well. Cover and leave to simmer for 15 to 20 minutes.

When cooked, the rice should be soft on the outside but with a slight bite to the inside. Stir the mushrooms into the risotto and remove the pan from the heat. Allow to cool.

Horizontally slice through each pork tenderloin, stopping about ½in from the edge, so that you do not cut right through. Open out and put it between 2 pieces of waxed paper and hit it with a rolling pin to flatten it. Do not hit it too hard or it will tear. Repeat with the remaining tenderloins. Season each piece of pork with salt and pepper. Divide the risotto mixture between the tenderloins, spreading it over the meat. Roll up each from one end and secure with 3 or 4 pieces of string. Heat the butter and vegetable oil in a large skillet over high heat. Add the stuffed tenderloins and brown them all over. Remove, leaving any juices in the pan, and transfer to a baking dish. Bake for 40 minutes, until the meat is cooked through.

To make the gravy, crush the half garlic clove into the juices left in the pan and fry for 30 seconds over medium heat. Stir in the flour and mix well. Increase the heat to high and pour in the sherry and stock, stirring to prevent lumps forming. Bring to a boil and boil for 4 to 5 minutes, until the gravy thickens and reduces slightly. Season and transfer to a warmed gravy boat.

Once the tenderloins are completely cooked, untie the string, and carve each into slices about 1 inch thick. Arrange the slices on a warmed serving platter. Serve immediately with the sherry gravy.

Indian Legend

The oldest Sanskrit manuscript dates from A.D. 350–375 and relates the Indian legend of the origins of garlic. Rahu, king of the Asuras, stole the elixir of life and drank it. The god Vishnu, however, sought revenge and cut off Rahu's head. Garlic sprang from the blood that was spilled.

CHAPTER FOUR

FISH

Among the huge variety of fish dishes from around the world, many are flavored with garlic. Whether it is cooked plainly or with spices, served with vegetables or alone, fish with a hint or more of garlic will always make a fragrant and welcome dish.

Fish

Garlic is a versatile flavoring for fish, whether used alone or mixed with other herbs, spices, and vegetables to make dishes of a highly individual character. Simmered first with chilies, spices, and coconut milk, garlic is the base for a Sri Lankan Tuna Fish Curry. *Mixed with dill and crème fraîche, it becomes a sauce with a Northern European flavor to accompany* Smoked Salmon Fish Cakes. *In Chinese style, a whole sea bass has slivers of garlic and ginger inserted into slits and is basted with soy sauce and vinegar during broiling.*

Fish can be baked in a variety of ways. Simply cooked fish dishes, such as broiled kabobs or fillets, benefit from a garlic-flavored marinade, or a rich garlic and tomato coulis. When it is wrapped in foil, all the flavors, including those of the garlic, are sealed into the package. When it is baked in a pie or on a bed of potatoes and garlic, there is a delicious mingling of flavors. For winter days try a warming Fish Stew *or a* Cod and Vegetable Crumble.

Kitchen Scene with Christ in the House of Martha and Mary, *Diego Velazques, 1618*

Smoked Salmon Fish Cakes *with* Garlic *and* Dill Sauce

Most people love fish cakes as children and forget about them when they become adults! However, fish cakes are easy to make and will be very welcome at any meal. The garlic sauce can be served with most fish, chicken, and vegetable dishes.

SERVES 4 (MAKES 8 FISH CAKES)

1¼lb potatoes, scrubbed, peeled, and cut into large cubes
1lb skinless white fish fillets, such as cod, flounder, or haddock
2tbsp butter, cut into small pieces
Salt and freshly ground black pepper
2 garlic cloves, crushed
1tbsp chopped fresh dill
3½oz smoked salmon, finely chopped
1 scallion, finely chopped
1 egg, beaten
2 cups fresh white bread crumbs
Oil for shallow frying

SAUCE
1tbsp butter
2 garlic cloves, finely chopped
1 cup crème fraîche
1tbsp chopped fresh dill
1tsp lemon juice
Salt and freshly ground black pepper

Put the potatoes in a large pan of lightly salted water and bring to a boil. Then reduce the heat and simmer for 10 to 15 minutes until the potatoes are just soft.

Wash and pat dry the fish fillets. Put them in the broiler pan, cover with half the butter, and season with pepper. Broil for 2 to 4 minutes until cooked through; set aside. Once cooled, flake the fillets and remove any remaining bones. Drain the potatoes and mash the flesh with the remaining butter. Add the flaked fish, garlic, dill, smoked salmon, onion, and seasoning, and mix well. Chill overnight or for at least an hour. Divide the mixture into 8 portions and roll each into a ball. Then put the balls on a lightly floured work surface and flatten them into cake shapes. Dip each cake in the egg and then coat it in the bread crumbs.

Heat the oil in a large skillet over medium heat and fry the fish cakes in 2 batches, for 2 to 3 minutes on each side, until they are crisp on the outside. Put aside and keep warm while you fry the second batch.

To make the sauce, melt the butter in a small saucepan over medium heat. Add the garlic and fry for 2 minutes, stirring frequently to prevent the garlic browning. Stir in the crème fraîche and cook until it melts; then add the remaining ingredients. Serve immediately.

Marinated Tuna Kabobs

Fresh tuna makes delicious kabobs. The garlic marinade quickly flavors the cubes of tuna and makes them wonderfully tender. These kabobs are fantastic cooked over a barbecue, accompanied by a green salad or new potatoes and green vegetables.

SERVES 4

14oz of tuna steak
16 small button mushrooms

MARINADE
3 garlic cloves, crushed
3tbsp olive oil
Grated peel and juice of 1 lemon
Grated peel and juice of 1 orange
1tbsp chopped fresh thyme or 1tsp dried thyme
Salt and freshly ground black pepper

Soak 8 wooden skewers in cold water for an hour, to prevent them from burning during cooking. Alternatively, use metal skewers. Wash and pat dry the tuna steak. Cut the steak into ¾-inch cubes and put the cubes in a nonmetallic bowl. Wipe the mushrooms and add them to the bowl. Combine the remaining ingredients and pour them over the tuna and mushrooms, tossing the cubes in the marinade to ensure they are all evenly coated. Cover and leave to marinate for 30 minutes to an hour in the refrigerator. Half-way through, toss the tuna and mushrooms again.

Thread the cubes of tuna and mushrooms onto the skewers, allowing 2 mushrooms per kabob. Preheat the broiler to high and oil the broiler rack. Brush the kabobs with the marinade and broil for 2 minutes on each side, brushing them with more of the marinade when you turn the kabobs. Serve immediately.

Garlic Festivals

Garlic festivals, both old and new, are held all over the world. One event which goes back to the Middle Ages is a celebration of aïoli monstre *(giant garlic mayonnaise), which is held every year in Provence. Garlic mayonnaise is served with fresh vegetables, bread, and red wine.*

In Cairo, there is an informal festival to celebrate the season's first green garlic, when the young plant is eaten with other green herbs and bread. Also in Egypt, there is a festival known as "sniffing the breezes" when garlic is eaten, worn, and crushed against doorframes and windowsills, echoing the age-old belief that garlic is a protection against evil influences.

In medieval Bologna, in Italy, on the Feast of St. John (June 24), everyone bought garlic to ensure the following year would be free from poverty.

The biggest garlic festival in the United States is the Gilroy Festival (see p.66), which is held each summer. In the fall, there is a garlic festival at Saugerties, on the Hudson River, 50 miles from New York City.

The Isle of Wight, off southern England, is home to the UK's only garlic festival. It has taken place since 1979 on the last weekend of August. Here you can sample garlic-flavored food, watch garlic cooking demonstrations, try garlic beer, and buy garlic in all its forms.

TROUT FILLETS *with* DOUBLE TOMATO COULIS

Coulis are uncooked or lightly cooked sauces which are amazingly fresh tasting. Although skinning and seeding tomatoes is time-consuming, it will make the coulis much easier to strain. Serve with boiled new potatoes and green vegetables.

SERVES 4

1tbsp olive oil
8 skinless trout fillets
1tbsp butter
1⅓ cups thinly sliced button mushrooms
1tsp sugar
Salt and freshly ground black pepper
6 pieces of sun-dried tomato in oil, drained and finely chopped
6 fresh basil leaves, roughly torn

COULIS
2tbsp olive oil
1 onion, very finely chopped
4 garlic cloves, crushed
3 cups skinned, seeded, and chopped ripe plum tomatoes

To make the coulis, heat the oil over medium heat and gently fry the onion in it for 3 to 4 minutes. Stir in the garlic and continue to fry genty for 2 minutes longer without browning the garlic. Next, add the chopped plum tomatoes, sugar, and seasoning. Cover and simmer for 30 minutes, stirring occasionally.

Next, push the tomato sauce through a strainer and return it to a clean pan. Add the sun-dried tomatoes and bring to a boil; then reduce the heat to a very gentle simmer.

While the coulis is simmering, heat the oil in a skillet and fry the trout fillets for 2 to 3 minutes on each side. Remove to a warmed serving dish and keep warm. Add the butter to the pan and gently sauté the mushrooms. Remove the coulis from the heat and stir in the basil leaves.

Serve each guest 2 trout fillets and 1 to 2 tablespoons of the coulis and top with some sautéed mushrooms.

GARLICKY MOULES *à la* MARINIÈRE

This is one of the most popular mussel dishes of all time. It is uncomplicated to prepare, although you need to allow enough time for cleaning the mussels before cooking. Only use mussels which are tightly closed or which close when tapped. Any that are cracked or open must be discarded, because they are already dead and can cause illness.

SERVES 4

4 quarts live mussels
2tbsp butter
1 onion, finely chopped
3 garlic cloves, finely chopped
4tbsp finely chopped fresh parsley
1¼ cups white wine
Salt and freshly ground black pepper
Crusty bread, to serve

First, rinse and scrub each mussel in plenty of cold water, removing the hairy "beard" from each. Change the water several times during cleaning and discard any mussels that are cracked or open. Put the mussels in a second bowl of water once they are cleaned. Drain and then run cold water over them to remove any remaining sand or grit.

Melt the butter in a large pan. Add the onion and garlic and fry for 5 to 6 minutes, until softened. Add 3 tablespoons of the parsley and the wine and bring to just below a boil. Add the mussels and cook for 1 to 2 minutes, covered. Shake the pan during cooking to speed up the cooking process. Using a slotted spoon, put the mussels in warmed serving dishes, discarding any that have not opened. (It may be necessary to cook the mussels in 2 batches if the pan is not large enough.)

Once all the mussels are cooked, increase the heat and reduce the liquid slightly. Check the seasoning, then strain the liquid—through cheesecloth if you have it—to remove any lingering sand or grit. Divide the liquid between the plates. Sprinkle with the remaining parsley and serve immediately, accompanied by plenty of crusty bread to mop up the delicious juices.

"Garlic is good to chew and fumigate."

AN ASSYRIAN HERBAL, 8TH CENTURY B.C.

FISH STEW *with* PASTRY LID

Most kinds of fish can be used for this dish as long as they do not have any skin or bones before you add them. The stew can be prepared in one large or four individual dishes and is topped with a golden puff-pastry lid. Serve with broccoli and peas, and remind your guests that there may still be whole garlic cloves in the stew!

SERVES 4

2tbsp olive oil
1tbsp butter
1 onion, finely chopped
8 garlic cloves, peeled and bruised
2 medium-size potatoes, peeled and cubed
2 medium-size leeks, cut into ½-in slices
1 cup fish or vegetable stock
1 cup dry white wine
⅔ cup light cream
2tbsp chopped fresh parsley
3 fresh thyme sprigs
1 to 1¼lb fresh fish, such as flounder, halibut, cod, salmon, or monkfish, cut into bite-size pieces
4oz jumbo shrimp, defrosted if frozen
3 squid tubes, prepared and cut into rings (optional)
Salt and freshly ground black pepper
8oz puff pastry dough, defrosted if frozen
Beaten egg, to glaze

Heat the oil and butter in a large saucepan over medium heat. Add the onion and gently sauté for about 5 minutes, until softened. Stir in the garlic and sauté for 1 minute longer. Add the potatoes and leeks and sauté for 2 minutes longer. Then pour in the stock and white wine. Bring to a boil. Reduce the heat and leave to simmer, covered, for 10 to 15 minutes, until the potatoes are tender.

Remove from the heat, add the cream, herbs, fish, shrimp, and squid (if using) and season well. Allow to cool completely and then transfer to an ovenproof casserole with a rim.

Meanwhile, prepare the puff pastry lid. Roll out the dough to about ¼ inch thick and cut a shape about 2 inches larger than the top of the casserole. Cut another strip of dough slightly wider than the rim of the dish and long enough to go all the way around.

Dampen the rim of the casserole with a finger or pastry brush dipped in water and put the strip of dough on it, joining the ends. Dampen the dough rim and position the lid loosely over the dish. Press the lid firmly onto the rim and trim as necessary. Crimp the edges together and, using the blade of a knife, knock up the edges of the pie, by gently tapping the edges of the dough together using a knife held horizontally. Decorate the pie with leaves made from the dough trimmings. Chill for 20 to 30 minutes. Preheat the oven to 400°F.

Make a couple of slits in the middle of the pie to allow steam to escape. Brush the pastry with beaten egg and bake for 25 to 30 minutes until the pastry is puffed and golden. If the pastry starts to brown too quickly, cover it loosely with foil. To make individual pies, divide the mixture between 4 ovenproof dishes and proceed as above, cutting 4 dough strips and lids to fit the dishes. Reduce the cooking time to 20 to 25 minutes.

Remedies for Garlic Smells

For all people's love of garlic, few enjoy the long-lasting smells that it produces. Here are a few quick solutions to those unwanted odors.

ANTIDOTES TO GARLIC BREATH

After you have eaten garlic, especially raw garlic, the odor is exhaled on your breath. You might not notice it, and nor might anyone else who has eaten the same meal, but those who have not shared the benefits of that delicious garlic dish may be on the receiving end of an unwanted side-effect. In theory, the more you eat garlic, the better your body is able to process it, and therefore the less its eventual effect on your breath. And if everybody ate garlic, then no one would find it objectionable! In the meantime, here are a few remedies:

An aromatherapist will tell you that rubbing neat peppermint oil on your feet will freshen your breath within 30 minutes. The oil is absorbed into the bloodstream and taken to the lungs, thus affecting the smell of your breath. (In the same way, rubbing garlic on the soles of your feet will give you garlic breath!) So when you have eaten garlic, combat the smell with the equally penetrating aroma of peppermint oil. Rub it on your feet and it will chase the garlic away.

Chlorophyll-rich plants are also said to be effective, so try chewing 1tbsp parsley or a raw green bean. Other recommended items to chew are ¼tsp caraway, 1 cardamom pod, ¼tsp aniseed, ¼tsp fennel seeds, a piece of apple, a coffee bean, and a slice of raw ginger. Modern remedies include chlorophyll tablets and mouthwashes that contain chloramine, peppermint essence or a chlorophyll product.

Fresh, green parsley is extremely effective for dealing with garlic smells: chew it for fresh breath or clean your hands with a mixture of parsley and lemon juice.

REMOVING SMELLS FROM A REFRIGERATOR

Readily available ingredients such as vanilla extract, peppermint oil, and lemons can be used as effective antidotes to garlic smells. This picture shows a potion being mixed in a 19th-century apothecary.

Put 2tbsp of baking soda into a small dish. Sprinkle 6 drops of vanilla extract on top and place the dish, uncovered, in the refrigerator. The garlic smell will disappear in about 12 hours and the refrigerator will remain odor-free until your next garlic dish is stored there.

HAND WASHES

Make a solution of ½tsp salt and the juice of half a lemon and rub it into your hands. Wash it off with soap and warm water. Alternatively, put ½ cup baking soda into a blender with the juice of 6 lemons and ½oz parsley and blend thoroughly. Keep the mixture in the refrigerator. After preparing garlic, rub a little of the mixture into your hands and then wash it off with soap and warm water.

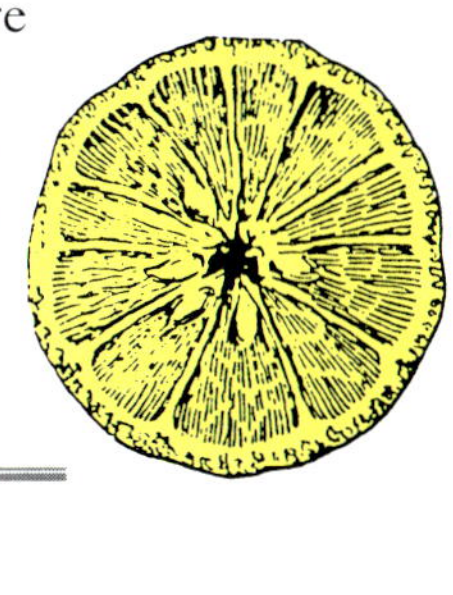

Spanish-Style Red Sea Bream

A whole red sea bream makes an impressive dinner-party centerpiece. It is a very tasty fish with plenty of white meat and goes well with garlic potatoes and onions. Although sea bream has many large bones, they are easy to remove.

SERVES 4

2tbsp butter
4tbsp olive oil
4 medium-size potatoes, thinly sliced
2 onions, thinly sliced
4 garlic cloves, thinly sliced
1 red sea bream, weighing 2 to 2½lb, scaled, gutted, and trimmed with the head removed
Salt and freshly ground black pepper
⅔ cup white wine

Preheat the oven to 400°F. Heat the butter and 1 tablespoon of oil in a large skillet and gently fry the potato slices in batches for 5 minutes, taking care not to break them up. Remove from the pan to a plate. Add the onions and garlic to the pan and fry gently for 5 minutes.

Lightly oil a baking dish or roasting pan and layer half the potato slices in it. Cover with half the onions and garlic. Put the prepared fish on top, season with salt and pepper and cover with the remaining onions, garlic, and potatoes. Season again and pour the white wine and remaining olive oil over. Cover with foil and bake for 30 minutes longer.

Remove the foil and bake for 10 minutes longer. Serve the fish and garlic potatoes and onions accompanied by grilled or broiled vegetables.

Chinese-Style Sea Bass *with* Ginger

Sea bass has an exquisite flavor and is an ideal fish to broil whole. Take the whole fish to the table for an impressive centerpiece. It is simple to serve as the flesh comes away easily and there are very few bones to worry about.

SERVES 4

1tbsp sesame or vegetable oil
1 sea bass, weighing 2 to 2½lb, gutted and scaled and with the gills removed
2 or 3 garlic cloves, finely sliced
1-in piece of fresh gingerroot, peeled and thinly sliced
3tbsp light soy sauce
2tbsp rice-wine vinegar
4 scallions, thinly shredded

Preheat the broiler to high. Line a broiler pan with foil and brush it with some of the oil. Wash and pat dry the sea bass and make 4 deep incisions diagonally across both sides. Put the sea bass in the broiler pan and insert half the slices of garlic and ginger into the stomach cavity. Put a slice of ginger or garlic in each slit. Combine the soy sauce and vinegar and pour half over the fish. Position the broiler pan about 4 inches away from the heat and broil the fish for 10 to 12 minutes, occasionally brushing it with oil and basting it with the soy sauce and vinegar.

Turn the fish over, put the remaining ginger and garlic in the slits, and pour the remaining soy sauce mixture over. Broil for 10 to 12 minutes longer. Turning the fish over without breaking it can be difficult, so use a couple of pancake turners or long serving implements.

Once cooked, carefully remove the fish to a warmed serving platter and scatter the shredded scallions on and around it. Serve immediately, accompanied by noodles or rice and stir-fried vegetables.

Egyptian Dentistry

The Egyptian Hesyt Re was Chief of Dentists and Physicians around 2600 B.C. The Egyptians did not like to have their teeth pulled out, no matter how rotten they were. To provide relief for the royal toothache, Re used to smear wild honey onto the pulp of a crushed garlic clove and use this to plug any cavities, the honey helping to stick the garlic in place.

Garlic for Natural Beauty

Nowadays, many people are becoming more aware that the cleansing and purifying properties of garlic can be put to good cosmetic use in a variety of potions and lotions.

Face Cleansers

Put 2oz lavender flowers into a blender. Add about 4 garlic cloves, the juice of 1 lemon and 2tbsp cider vinegar and blend thoroughly. Leave in a refrigerator to thicken, then apply to the face with a cotton ball. Rinse off with lukewarm water and then splash some cool water on your face to refresh the skin. Alternatively, mix the juice of 1 lemon with 2 crushed garlic cloves and 4tbsp warm water. Apply the mixture to your face with a cotton ball. Wash off with lukewarm water and then splash your face with cold water to refresh. Both of these cleansers are particularly suitable for oily skin.

The Cosmetic Benefits of Eating Garlic

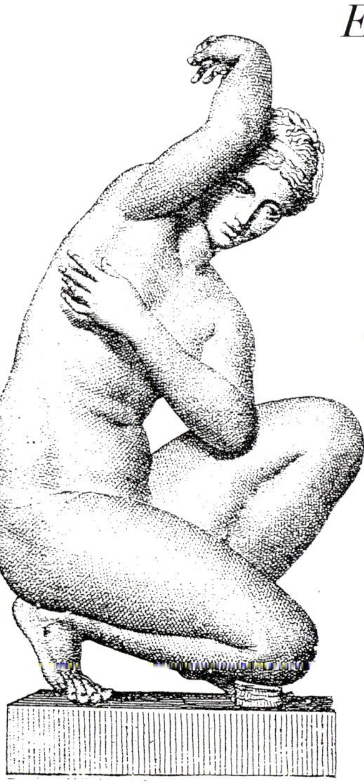

Eat garlic regularly for clear, unblemished skin.

Drink a garlic infusion made by adding 1 garlic clove to 1 cup boiling water. Leave this covered until it cools and then strain it. This infusion aids circulation and will therefore help to smooth away wrinkles.

Eat garlic to promote hair growth, improve its condition, and help to get rid of dandruff.

Scalp and Hair Lotions

Crush the cloves from 1 bulb fresh garlic and steep them in ½ cup vodka for 3 days. Filter the liquid and add an equal amount of water. Add 4 drops rosemary oil.

Once a week, after washing and drying your hair, massage the lotion gently into your scalp and brush it through your hair with a soft brush, making your hair damp but not wet.

Baths of Caracalla, *Lawrence Alma-Tadema, 19th century. Garlic has long been associated with purification and cleansing. Using garlic-based beauty products, as well as eating garlic, will help you to keep a clear, unblemished complexion and will give you shiny, healthy hair.*

PRAWNS *in* PERNOD *with* FRESH PASTA

When you are at a loss for something new to do with pasta, this unusual but delicious recipe is well worth a try. The prawns are flambéed in Pernod, which gives them a wonderful aniseed flavor. It is quick to make and is ideal as a first course, a main course or a rather special light lunch.

SERVES 4

200g • 7oz angel-hair (thin spaghetti) pasta, fresh or dried
90g • 3oz butter
6 spring onions, thinly sliced
2 garlic cloves, crushed
2tsp fennel seeds
500g • 1lb raw tiger prawns, defrosted if frozen and peeled
3tbsp Pernod
Salt and freshly ground black pepper

Cook the pasta in a large pan of boiling water for approximately 8 minutes if fresh or 12 minutes if dried. Drain and place in a warmed serving dish.

To make the sauce, melt 45g (1½oz) of the butter in a frying-pan, add the spring onions and cut the remaining butter into small pieces. Gently fry the spring onions for 1 minute, then add the garlic and fennel seeds and cook for a further 2 minutes. Stir in the prawns and cook for 2 to 3 minutes, until pink. Pour the Pernod into a cup or small jug, tip it into the frying-pan and quickly set light to it. Be careful when doing this and pull your hand away quickly. Allow the flames to die down. Add the small pieces of butter and allow them to melt, whisking to incorporate the butter into the sauce. Season with salt and pepper.

Top the cooked pasta with the Pernod prawns and the sauce and serve immediately, accompanied by a green salad

"What do you think? Young women of rank eat – you will never guess what – garlick!"

THE SHOCKED ROMANTIC POET SHELLEY IN A LETTER TO A FRIEND AFTER A VISIT TO FRANCE, 1810S

RED MULLET *baked with* MEDITERRANEAN VEGETABLES

It is best to bake the red mullet livers intact, as this is where most of the flavor comes from during cooking. This is a quick dish to make, as you can prepare any accompanying vegetables while the fish is baking. The ideal accompaniments are new potatoes and a green vegetable.

SERVES 4

4 red mullet, each weighing about 430g • 14oz, scaled and gutted, if preferred
3tbsp olive oil
1 fennel head, thinly sliced
4 garlic cloves, sliced
1 large beef tomato, thinly sliced
4 fresh oregano sprigs
Salt and freshly ground black pepper

Preheat the oven to 200°C/400°F/gas mark 6. Cut four squares of foil, each large enough to enclose one fish, and brush each one with some of the oil. Put a couple of slices of fennel in the middle of each foil square and place a fish on top. Top each fish with one sliced garlic clove, two slices of tomato and some more slices of fennel. Scatter over the leaves from a sprig of oregano and sprinkle on the remaining olive oil. Season with salt and pepper.

Draw up the sides of the foil squares and crimp the edges together to form a loose parcel. Put all the parcels on a baking sheet and bake them in the oven for approximately 25 to 30 minutes.

To serve, remove the fish and vegetables from the parcels and arrange them on individual plates.

COD *and* VEGETABLE CRUMBLE

This is the perfect dish for a family supper. It has a warming fish and vegetable filling and a delightfully crunchy, nutty topping. Serve it with mashed potato and green vegetables.

SERVES 4 TO 6

2½ cups lowfat milk
1 to 1½lb skinless cod fillets
1tbsp olive or vegetable oil
3 cups thinly sliced leeks
3 garlic cloves, crushed
1½ cups quartered button mushrooms
1 cup canned corn kernels
½ cup frozen peas
Salt and freshly ground black pepper
3tbsp butter
⅓ cup all-purpose flour
3tbsp finely chopped fresh parsley

TOPPING
2 cups fresh white or whole-wheat bread crumbs
¾ cup grated cheddar cheese
½ cup finely chopped nuts, such as hazlenuts, peanuts or walnuts, or slivered almonds, roughly chopped
Salt and freshly ground black pepper
1tbsp butter, cut into small pieces

Put the milk in a saucepan over medium heat and add the cod fillets. Just as the first bubbles appear, remove the pan from the heat, turn each fillet over and leave to cool in the milk. Once the fish is cool, lift out each piece with a slotted spoon. Reserve the remaining milk for the sauce.

Preheat the oven to 375°F. Heat the oil in a saucepan and gently fry the leeks for 5 minutes, until soft. Stir in the garlic and fry for one minute longer, without browning the garlic. Add the mushrooms, corn, and peas and cook for a few minutes longer. Remove from the heat and season.

To make the sauce, melt the butter in a small saucepan. Add the flour, mix well, and cook for a minute. Gradually add the reserved milk, stirring constantly to prevent lumps from forming. Once all the milk is mixed in, stir in the parsley and seasoning and then mix the sauce into the vegetables. Break the fish into chunks and fold them carefully into the vegetable mixture.

Combine all the topping ingredients in a bowl, with the exception of the butter. Lightly oil a baking dish and pour in the fish mixture. Sprinkle the topping over and dot with the butter. Bake for 30 to 35 minutes, or until the topping is golden. Serve immediately.

If you prefer, make the filling the day before and cover with the crumble topping just before baking.

TUNA-FISH CURRY *with* COCONUT SAMBAL

Fish curries are very popular in Sri Lanka, where one meal can include up to eight different curries accompanied by a host of chutneys, relishes, and sambals. A sambal is a simple-to-prepare spicy relish; coconut sambal is probably the most common. Serve this dish with boiled rice and poppadoms and a selection of chutneys and relishes.

SERVES 4

4 fresh tuna steaks
Juice of 1 lime
3 garlic cloves, finely chopped
1 small onion, finely chopped
2 or 3 fresh green chilies, seeded and finely chopped
½-in piece of fresh gingerroot, finely chopped
½tsp ground fenugreek
2tsp ground coriander
½tsp ground cumin
½ cinnamon stick
1tsp chili powder
1tsp curry powder
Pinch of salt
1¾ cups coconut milk

SAMBAL

1 red onion, finely chopped
2 dried red chilies, seeded and finely chopped
Juice of 1 lime
¾ cup freshly grated coconut, or ½ cup shredded coconut with 1 or 2tbsp of warm milk added to soften it
1tsp salt

Wash and pat dry the fish steaks and cut them into chunks. Put the pieces in a bowl, sprinkle them with the lime juice and mix well.

Put all the other curry ingredients in a saucepan and bring to a boil, then reduce the heat and leave to simmer for 3 minutes, uncovered. Add the fish to the pan and leave to simmer for 10 minutes longer.

To make the sambal, combine all the ingredients in a small bowl and transfer them to a small serving dish.

Once the curry is cooked, remove the cinnamon stick and serve, accompanied by the coconut sambal.

"I have been spending some weeks of dissipation in London, and was transformed by Circe's cup, not into a brute, but a beau. I am now eating herb Moly in the country."

SYDNEY SMITH, 18TH–19TH-CENTURY WIT AND ESSAYIST

AVAL DE GARANTIA
COOPERAT
VIRGEN DE
CALASP

CHAPTER FIVE

DRESSINGS AND SAUCES

Specially made dressings, marinades, and sauces add a magic touch to the simplest dish. Use the best-quality ingredients, add a little chopped, crushed, or puréed garlic, and your meal will be fit for a king.

Dressings and Sauces

Slice or chop some raw vegetables and make a dressing of fine-quality olive oil, wine vinegar and garlic, adding, if you wish, fresh herbs and a little mustard. Combine the vegetables and the dressing, and you have the perfect salad. If you like your dressing to be rich and thick, make Aïoli, *the garlic-flavored mayonnaise traditionally served in Provence. Garlic is an important ingredient in many dips. Some are cool and refreshing, such as the Greek* Tzatziki *made with yogurt and cucumber, others are rich and sizzling like* Bagna Cauda, *an anchovy dip from the Piedmont area of Italy. Many plainly cooked dishes taste their best when served with a sauce. Try a* Rich Tomato and Garlic Sauce *or a light, creamy one made with stock, white wine, and cream. Spicy dishes from eastern countries are often served with a small portion of garlic-flavored chutney or sambal on the side, which acts as a contrast to the richly sauced meats and vegetables. A garlic-flavored marinade will tenderize and flavor meat or fish. Mix crushed garlic with the fresh flavors of citrus juices, or combine it more robustly with red wine, vegetables, and herbs.*

Banquet scene from the Luttrell Psalter, English, 1340

AÏOLI (GARLIC MAYONNAISE)

Aïoli is a traditional Provençal dish, which can be eaten simply with a few raw vegetables or can be made into a feast with chicken, snails, fish, boiled potatoes, and lightly cooked vegetables. Alternatively, use it as a simple garlic mayonnaise in sandwiches and with salads. Aïoli keeps for a week in the refrigerator.

MAKES ABOUT 1¼ CUPS

4 garlic cloves, quartered
Pinch of salt
2 egg yolks
1¼ cups vegetable or olive oil
1tbsp lemon juice
Pinch of white pepper

The traditional method of making aïoli is with a mortar and pestle, adding a drop of oil at a time and then slowly increasing the speed at which the oil is added. However, as most people now have an electric mixer or food processor, it is so much easier to use this instead. First, make sure all the ingredients are at room temperature. Put the garlic and a little salt in a medium-size bowl and mix together. Add the egg yolks and mix them well with the garlic. Next, with the mixer or food processor in motion, start to add the oil very slowly, in drops, blending the mixture well before adding more oil. Always keep the whisk or food processor in motion and continue to add the oil drop by drop until the mayonnaise starts to thicken.

As the mayonnaise starts to bind, add the oil in larger drops, but always ensure all the oil is incorporated before adding any more. Once you have added half the oil in drops, you can add the rest in a slow, steady stream. Continue blending until all the oil is used up and the mayonnaise is thick and creamy. Then stir in the lemon juice and a pinch of white pepper. If the mayonnaise starts to curdle at any time, beat in 1 to 2 teaspoons of boiling water. If this fails, put another egg yolk in a clean bowl and very slowly add the curdled mixture, one drop at a time; then continue as above. The garlic flavor of the mayonnaise will intensify the longer it is left to stand.

GARLICKY VINAIGRETTE *with* FRESH HERBS

Nothing peps up a bowl of salad leaves better than a good-quality vinaigrette dressing. Dress the leaves just before serving to prevent them becoming soggy.

MAKES ABOUT ½ CUP

6tbsp extra-virgin olive oil
2tbsp white-wine vinegar or 1½tbsp balsamic vinegar
2 garlic cloves, halved
1tsp coarse-grain mustard
2tsp finely chopped fresh herbs, such as basil, oregano, parsley, and chives
Salt and freshly ground black pepper

Place all the ingredients in a screw-topped jar and shake well. Leave for a couple of hours before using to allow the dressing to absorb the flavor of the garlic. Discard the garlic before serving.

To have a delicious garlic dressing available at all times, make three or four times the quantity above, adding just 2 garlic cloves, halved. It will keep for several weeks if stored in a screw-top jar in a dark cupboard. Shake well before using and make sure the garlic cloves remain in the jar when the dressing is poured out.

Household Uses of Garlic

Garlic cloves in drawers and cupboards can keep moths away.

If you run out of paper glue, garlic makes a good substitute. Rub both pieces of paper to be glued with a cut clove of garlic. Press them until the juice dries and sticks them together.

MANGO *and* GARLIC CHUTNEY

Chutneys are ideal for serving with curries, cold meats, and cheeses. This chutney also makes an ideal sandwich filling, with ham or cheese and salad. To sterilize the jars for the chutney, stand them on a wire rack in a saucepan and cover with water. Cover the pan and boil for 15 minutes. Just before sealing, dip any lids or seals in the boiling water to sterilize them.

MAKES ABOUT 3 CUPS

2¼ cups cider vinegar
2½ cups sugar
5 garlic cloves, finely chopped
1-in piece of fresh gingerroot, peeled and finely chopped
2 large, firm mangoes, roughly chopped
⅓ cup dried apricots, roughly chopped
⅔ cup raisins

Place the vinegar and sugar in a heavy-bottomed saucepan and bring to a boil, stirring frequently until the sugar has dissolved. Reduce the heat, add the remaining ingredients and simmer, uncovered, for 15 minutes, until the mango is tender. Using a slotted spoon, put the fruit in a bowl and reserve. Increase the heat, bring the syrup back to a boil and cook for 10 to 15 minutes longer, until the syrup is thick and reduced by about half. Return the fruit to the pan and bring the syrup back to a boil. Transfer the chutney to sterilized jars and seal them.

SRI LANKAN SAMBAL

Sambals are similar to chutneys and relishes and are served as accompaniments to Sri Lankan meals. This sambal is suitable for serving with curries, cold meats, and cheeses.

MAKES ABOUT 1 CUP

2tbsp vegetable oil
2 onions, sliced into thin half-rings
1 eggplant (about 8oz), sliced into thin half-rings
2 large garlic cloves, finely chopped
¼tsp ground turmeric
2tsp chili powder

Heat the oil in a large, heavy-bottomed saucepan. Add the onion rings and eggplant and fry very gently for about 10 minutes without allowing them to burn. Stir in the garlic, and fry for 5 minutes longer. Add the turmeric and chili powder, mix well and cook for 10 minutes longer, until the mixture has reduced and thickened slightly. Transfer to a bowl and leave to cool.

"Sith garlicke then hath power to save from death,
Beare with it though it makes unsavoury breath;
And scorn not garlicke, like to some that thinke,
It only makes men winke, and drinke and stinke."

SIR JOHN HARRINGTON,
THE ENGLISH DOCTOR, 1609

RICH TOMATO *and* GARLIC SAUCE

This sauce is ideal for making in the summer, if there is a glut of tomatoes. It freezes well and can be served with pasta, meat, fish, and vegetables.

MAKES ABOUT 2½ CUPS

2tbsp olive oil
1 onion, finely chopped
3 garlic cloves, crushed
1½lb fresh plum or other tomatoes, chopped
¾ cup vegetable stock or water
1tsp sugar (optional)
Salt and freshly ground black pepper
4 fresh basil leaves, roughly torn

Heat the oil in a medium-size saucepan and add the onion. Cook over medium heat for 5 minutes. Stir in the garlic and cook for 3 minutes longer, until the onions are softened.

Add the chopped tomatoes, stock or water, sugar, if using, and seasoning. Bring to a boil. Reduce the heat to a simmer and leave to cook, covered, for 50 minutes, stirring occasionally. Remove the lid and simmer for 10 minutes longer, until the sauce is rich and thickened. Check the seasoning, stir in the basil leaves and serve.

GARLIC MARINADE

This marinade is suitable for pork, chicken, and fish. It is also perfect for basting meat and fish during cooking and can be added to any accompanying sauces.

MAKES ENOUGH TO MARINATE ABOUT 1LB MEAT

4tbsp olive oil
4 garlic cloves, crushed
Juice of 1 orange
Juice of 1 lime
2tbsp finely chopped fresh parsley
Salt and freshly ground black pepper

Combine all the ingredients in a bowl. If using cubes or strips of meat or fish, toss them in the marinade and leave for at least 30 minutes; then use the marinade as a baste during cooking.

If using larger pieces of meat, make several incisions across the surface of the meat, put it in a shallow dish, pour the marinade over, cover, and leave for 1 to 2 hours.

If using larger pieces of fish, simply pour the marinade over, cover, and leave to marinate for 30 minutes.

Sirrop of Garlick: My First Cousen Clerkes

Take three heads of garlick and peele of the upper skine, then boyle them in a little whitewine while the strength of them be something abated, then take two quarts of whitewine, one handfull of red sage; as much of heartshorne [hartshorn], and as much of unset Isopp [hyssop], then take your garlick; pick every clove that the strength may come forth, put them altogether into the wine, so let them boyle gently untill they come to a quart, then take a pounde of the best honny and put to it, affter the honny is in let it but just boyle up that so you may scume it, then strayne it all, this sirrop is rear good for a Tisike [tisick], and for a colde, and a cough, take of it one spoonefull at a time, (or two if you please) in ye morning fasting, and at foure of the Clock in the affternoone, and at going to bed at night; this sirrop is also good for a consumtion.

REBECCA PRICE,
THE COMPLEAT COOK, 17TH CENTURY

RED-WINE *and* GARLIC MARINADE

This is a rich marinade, which can be used to enhance the flavor of beef, game, poultry, or pork.

MAKES 2 CUPS

3tbsp olive oil
3 garlic cloves, thinly sliced
1 onion, sliced
1 carrot, sliced
1 celery stick, sliced
2½ cups red wine
4tbsp red-wine vinegar
6 juniper berries, lightly crushed
1 bay leaf
2 sprigs of fresh thyme
Salt and freshly ground black pepper
1tbsp cornstarch

Heat the oil in a saucepan and gently fry the garlic, onion, carrot, and celery for 10 minutes, until softened. Add the remaining ingredients and bring to a boil. Reduce the heat and simmer for 15 minutes. Remove from the heat and allow to cool. Pour the liquid through a strainer into a bowl, squeezing out as much liquid as possible. Place any meat to be marinated in a plastic container (or other container that will not react with the marinade) and pour the marinade over. Ensure all the meat is covered with the liquid, cover, and leave in the refrigerator for at least 24 hours and up to 72 hours. Turn and baste the meat occasionally. Once marinated, remove the meat and cook it.

The marinade can be used as a rich accompanying sauce. Simply pour it into a saucepan, place over high heat and boil rapidly, to reduce the sauce by a quarter. Then mix 1 tablespoon of cornstarch with 1 tablespoon of water and stir the mixture into the pan. Continue boiling until the sauce has thickened. Serve with the meat.

Garlic Around the World

Garlic is an important cooking ingredient in cuisines throughout the world. It is used in many different ways to enhance the flavor of regional dishes, and most countries have created their own garlic specialities.

Caribbean

Garlic is a relative newcomer to the Caribbean islands. A favorite garlic-based recipe is *blaff*, from Martinique. This consists of fish marinated in lime juice and salt and poached in a thick court bouillon flavored with onions, garlic, chilies, bay rum berries, and lime.

United States

Garlic was brought to the United States by settlers from many lands, so the country's garlic cuisine is multinational. One of the most popular "home-grown" garlic dishes is the Pepper-Steak Sandwich. It is said that missionaries first took garlic to California; now that state grows 90 percent of the U.S. crop and supplies garlic worldwide.

Great Britain

Great Britain has come to love garlic, thanks to increased foreign travel and to immigrants from all over the Commonwealth who brought with them their cooking styles and foods. There is nott a classic British garlic dish, but there are few restaurants and country pubs without garlic mushrooms or garlic bread on the menu.

Spain

A once common sight in northern Spain was the itinerant garlic and chili pepper seller, who traveled the country carrying huge strings of white garlic bulbs and dried red chilies on his shoulders. The simplest use of garlic in Spain is one of the most delicious. Take a thick slice of new, crusty white bread, rub it with a cut tomato and then with a cut clove of garlic, and enjoy the taste.

South America

Garlic was taken to South America by the Spanish and Portuguese in the 16th century, and became integrated into much of the continent's cooking. It is used in sauces and salsas, in chili paste, and in fillings for tortillas.

Africa

One of the main uses for garlic in Africa is to make *berbere*, the fiery hot paste from Ethiopia that serves as a seasoning in cooked dishes and as a dip for plain bread. Red peppers are dried in the sun and pounded in a mortar. Garlic and ginger are pounded together, added to the peppers, and all are mixed and pounded again with salt, onions, and many other spices to make a thick, red purée.

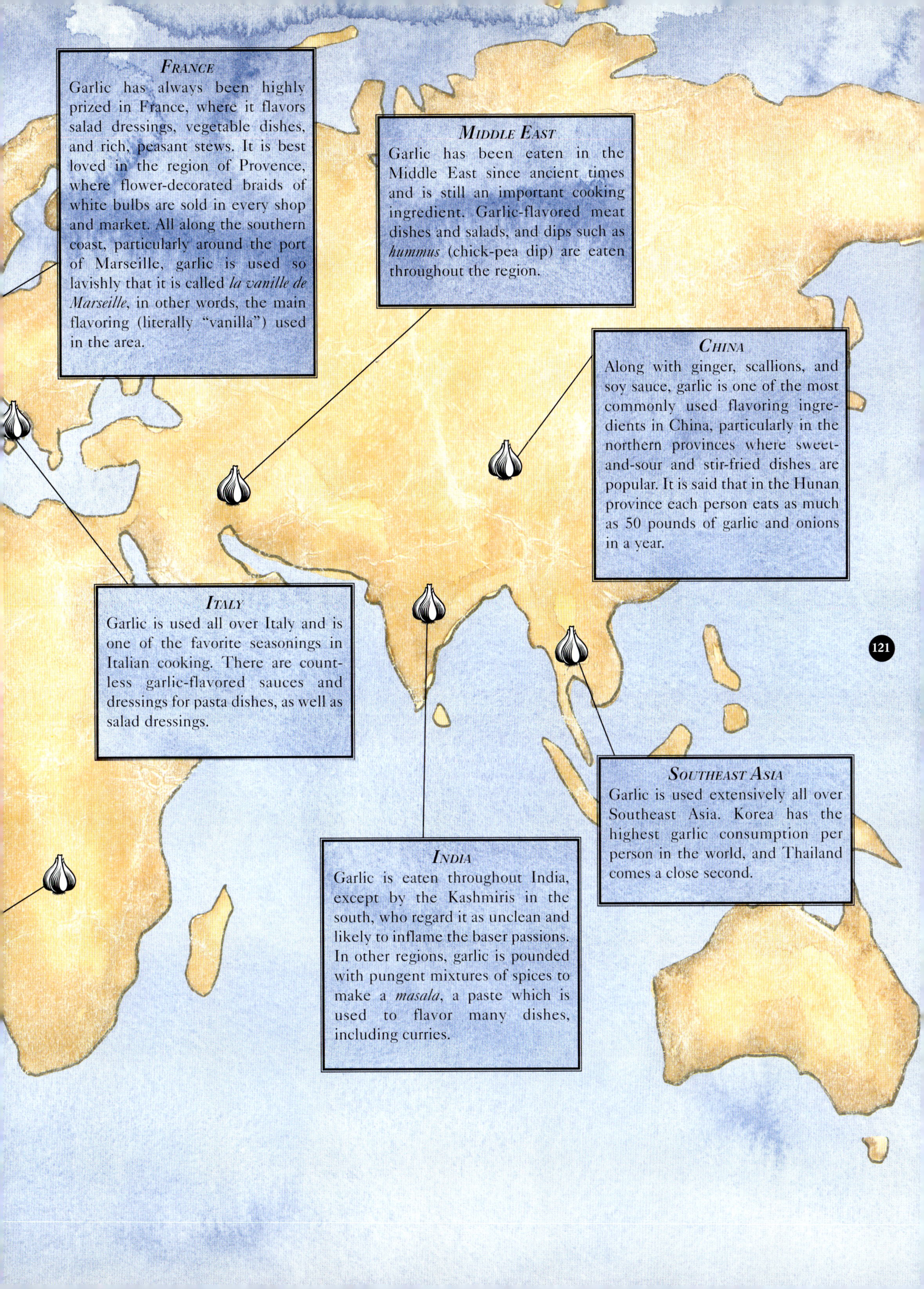

France

Garlic has always been highly prized in France, where it flavors salad dressings, vegetable dishes, and rich, peasant stews. It is best loved in the region of Provence, where flower-decorated braids of white bulbs are sold in every shop and market. All along the southern coast, particularly around the port of Marseille, garlic is used so lavishly that it is called *la vanille de Marseille*, in other words, the main flavoring (literally "vanilla") used in the area.

Middle East

Garlic has been eaten in the Middle East since ancient times and is still an important cooking ingredient. Garlic-flavored meat dishes and salads, and dips such as *hummus* (chick-pea dip) are eaten throughout the region.

China

Along with ginger, scallions, and soy sauce, garlic is one of the most commonly used flavoring ingredients in China, particularly in the northern provinces where sweet-and-sour and stir-fried dishes are popular. It is said that in the Hunan province each person eats as much as 50 pounds of garlic and onions in a year.

Italy

Garlic is used all over Italy and is one of the favorite seasonings in Italian cooking. There are countless garlic-flavored sauces and dressings for pasta dishes, as well as salad dressings.

Southeast Asia

Garlic is used extensively all over Southeast Asia. Korea has the highest garlic consumption per person in the world, and Thailand comes a close second.

India

Garlic is eaten throughout India, except by the Kashmiris in the south, who regard it as unclean and likely to inflame the baser passions. In other regions, garlic is pounded with pungent mixtures of spices to make a *masala*, a paste which is used to flavor many dishes, including curries.

TZATZIKI *with* GREEN PEPPER

A traditional Greek dip for serving with pita bread and crudités. Although green pepper is not a traditional ingredient, it gives the dip a crunchy texture and also adds welcome color.

MAKES 1¼ CUPS

1tbsp olive oil
2tsp lemon juice
2 garlic cloves, crushed
1 cup thick plain yogurt
½ cup peeled and finely chopped cucumber
½ green bell pepper, seeded and finely chopped
Salt and freshly ground black pepper

Combine the oil and lemon juice in a bowl and stir in the garlic. Gradually beat in the yogurt, ensuring that it mixes well with the oil. Stir in the cucumber and green pepper and season. Leave in the refrigerator to chill. The longer this dip is left, the more intense the garlic flavor will become. Serve with pita bread and crudités.

BAGNA CAUDA

This is a traditional Italian sauce from the Piedmont region. Serve it hot, as a dip for raw vegetables.

MAKES ABOUT 1 CUP

½ cup butter
3tbsp olive oil
4 garlic cloves, crushed
2-oz can of anchovy fillets, drained and finely chopped
Raw vegetables, to serve

Heat the butter and oil in a small saucepan over gentle heat. Stir in the crushed garlic and cook gently for 2 minutes, without browning. Add the anchovies and cook for 10 minutes longer, stirring constantly until the anchovies dissolve into a paste.

Put the dip in a warmed serving dish and keep it warm at the table over a fondue burner or candle burner. Serve a selection of crisp fresh vegetables, such as carrots, peppers, cauliflower, and celery, for dipping into the sauce.

CREAMY GARLIC *and* WHITE WINE SAUCE

This is a delicious, all-purpose sauce for serving with pasta, vegetables, chicken, pork, or fish. To make a simple, but mouthwatering appetizer, simply sauté some button mushrooms and stir them into the sauce. Serve with plenty of crusty bread to mop up the sauce.

MAKES ABOUT 1¼ CUPS

1tbsp olive oil
2 shallots, finely chopped
3 garlic cloves, finely chopped
2tbsp all-purpose flour
⅔ cup chicken or vegetable stock
⅔ cup dry white wine
5tbsp light cream
Salt and freshly ground black pepper

Heat the oil in a saucepan and add the shallots. Cook over medium heat for 3 minutes. Then stir in the garlic and cook for 2 minutes longer, until the garlic is softened. Add the flour and mix well, scraping any bits from the bottom of the pan. Cook for 1 minute. Pour in the stock and wine a little at a time, stirring rapidly and constantly until the sauce becomes smooth. Increase the heat and bring to a boil. Continue boiling until the sauce has reduced by a quarter, stirring frequently. Then stir in the cream and seasoning and heat through. Serve immediately.

Garlic – Broad-Leaved Wild

DESCRIPTION—*The root of this is round and whitish; the leaves are oblong, very broad, of a fine deep green. The stalk of a pale green, three square, and ten inches high, whereon grow small white flowers.*

PLACE—*It is common in damp woods in the western counties.*

TIME—*It flowers in April.*

GOVERNMENT AND VIRTUES—*It is under Mars as well as the former. The root is only known in physic; it is a powerful opener, and on account of its subtle parts, in which it abounds, discussive: it seldom agrees with dry constitutions, but it performs almost miracles in phlegmatic habits of body. It wonderfully opens the lungs, and gives relief in asthmas; nor is it without its merit in wind colics; and is a good diuretic, which appears by the smell it communicates to the urine. It is very useful in obstructions of the kidneys, and dropsies, especially in that which is called anasarca. It may be taken in a morning fasting, or else the conserve of garlic which is kept in the shops may be used.*

NICHOLAS CULPEPER,
THE ENGLISH PHYSICIAN, c.1640

Five Ideas for Garlic Purée

Some recipes in this book call for garlic purée, made by roasting a whole head of garlic for 30 to 35 minutes at 325°F and then squeezing out the softened flesh of the cloves. Use as much or as little of the purée as you wish in these recipes, remembering that the pungent flavor of garlic is greatly reduced when it has been roasted.

Goat Cheese, Walnut, and Thyme Spread

This spread is delicious served as an appetizer and can be prepared well in advance for a special meal.

MAKES ABOUT ¾ CUP

Garlic purée (see above)
5oz soft goat cheese
1tbsp finely chopped fresh thyme or 2tsp dried thyme
2tbsp olive oil
Salt and freshly ground black pepper
¼ cup finely chopped walnut pieces

Place all the ingredients, except the walnuts, in a bowl and mash them together with a fork. Stir in the walnuts and serve with triangles of toast or warm pita bread.

Garlic and Eggplant Dip

The roasted eggplant gives a rich, smoky flavor to this delicious garlic dip.

MAKES ABOUT 1 CUP

1 large eggplant
Garlic purée (see above)
3tbsp olive oil
2tbsp chopped fresh parsley
Salt and freshly ground black pepper

Prick the eggplant a couple of times with a fine skewer and bake for 40 minutes at 375°F. Let the eggplant cool slightly and then cut it into thick slices. Put the slices in a food processor, with the remaining ingredients and blend them until smooth. Serve with crudités, triangles of toast and bread sticks.

Mediterranean Pâté

Sun-drenched flavors from the Mediterranean combine in an easy-to-make pâté.

MAKES ABOUT 1LB

Garlic purée (see above left)
16 pitted ripe olives, chopped
7oz feta cheese, crumbled
4 pieces of sun-dried tomato in oil, chopped
1tbsp olive oil
3tbsp crème fraîche

Place all the ingredients in a blender or food processor and blend them together for a couple of seconds (the mixture should still be a bit lumpy). Line 4 small ramekins with plastic wrap and spoon the mixture into them, then cover and chill. To serve, carefully turn out the pâté molds and serve them with toast or bread sticks.

Garlicky Guacamole with Chilies

The perfect accompaniment to Mexican and other spicy foods, this is cooling and refreshing, despite the chili.

MAKES ABOUT 1 CUP

Garlic purée (see above left)
1 large ripe avocado
2tsp lemon juice
1 red chili, seeded and chopped
3tbsp soured cream

Place all the ingredients in a blender or food processor and blend them until smooth. Serve with tortilla chips and a variety of crudités.

Garlic and Chick-pea Dip

The flavors of garlic and chick-peas combine beautifully in this Middle-Eastern inspired dip.

MAKES ABOUT 1½ CUPS

Garlic purée (see above left)
14-oz can of chick-peas
6tbsp olive oil
Salt and freshly ground black pepper
1tbsp chopped fresh herbs or 2tsp Italian seasoning
2tbsp lemon juice
2tbsp crème fraîche (optional)

Place all the ingredients in a blender or food processor and blend them until smooth. Serve with a variety of crudités and pita bread.

General Index

Italics refer to illustration captions

Index *of* Recipes

Credits

Key: *a* above; *b* below; *c* center; *l* left; *r* right

Harry Smith Horticultural Collection 6; ET Archive 7, 8 & 9*a*; PLI/Ace Photo Agency 9b; Mansell Collection 10*a*; The Stinking Rose Restaurant, San Francisco CA 10*b*; ET Archive 11*a* & *b*; Mansell Collection 11*c*; J Allan Cash 12*al*; Ann Ronan at Image Select 12*cr*; ET Archive 13*a* & *b*; Ann Ronan at Image Select 14; Mansell Collection 16*a* & *b*; J Allan Cash 16*c*; PictureBank 17*al*; AA Photo Library 17*c*; J Allan Cash 17*b*; Pictor 18, 19 & 20; Ann Ronan at Image Select 21*bl*; ET Archive 21*br*; Ann Ronan at Image Select 22*a*; Harry Smith Horticultural Collection 22*b*; Christopher Ranch, Gilroy CA 23*a*; PictureBank 24*a*; Harry Smith Horticultural Collection 24*c*; ET Archive 24*b*; Mansell Collection 25*l*; ET Archive 25*r* & 27*b*; Culpeper, London 28*a*; Wellcome Institute Library, London 28*b*; Mansell Collection 32*l* & *c*; Image Select 33*a*; ET Archive 33*bl*; Fortean Picture Library 34*b*; ET Archive 35*l*; Ann Ronan at Image Select 35*r*; Fortean Picture Library 36*a* & *b*; ET Archive 37*a* & *b*; Visual Arts Library 43; ET Archive 61; Christopher Ranch, Gilroy CA 67; Visual Arts Library 81; Fortean Picture Library 90; ET Archive 91*a*; Mansell Collection 91*b*; The National Gallery, London 97; ET Archive 103*a*; Harry Smith Horticultural Collection 103*b*; Carlos Navajas/Image Bank 106*a*; Northwind Picture Archive 106*b*; ET Archive 106*c* & 113

Author's acknowledgments (KH)
I would like to thank my family and friends for all their help during the writing and testing of the recipes in this book, in particular Tim, Sue, Iqbal, Tina and Tony, Richard and Claire, Liz and Justin, Emma, Simon and Lisa, and my parents for their neverending support.